Dear Miss Cusek:

Hope that this may help to ease the pain and shorten the hours while you are hospitalized.

Wishing you a speedy recovery and hope to see you back at your desk real soon.

Sincerely

Mae T. Holzer

Room 3435

LAUGHING STOCK

Laughing Stock

Over Six-hundred Jokes and
Anecdotes of Uncertain Vin-
tage; Edited by

Bennett Cerf

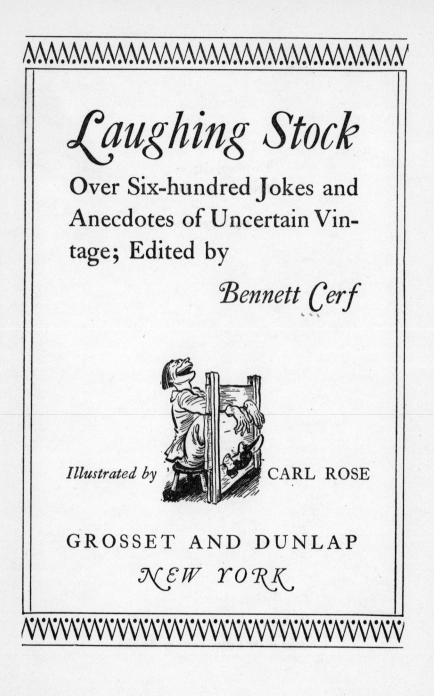

Illustrated by   CARL ROSE

GROSSET AND DUNLAP
NEW YORK

∧∧∧∧∧∧∧∧∧∧∧∧∧∧∧∧∧∧∧∧∧∧∧∧∧∧∧∧∧

Introduction

IN TIMES LIKE THESE, when anything in book form that re-
motely resembles humor is selling like hotcakes (by the way, do
you know anybody who ever actually *bought* a hotcake?), and
when a dozen top-line radio comics are beating out their brains in
search of new gags to make the customers give with the chuckles,
the man who is fortunate enough to have a good memory for
jokes and witticisms is worth his weight in gold, and even paper.

(v)

I've had a weakness for funny stories ever since I was a kid in the Pulitzer School of Journalism, so this is my lucky day. I fell into the editorship of the Columbia Jester in my sophomore year because the previous pilot had been kicked out for "editorial indiscretions." (He won a Pulitzer Prize some years later.) I ran afoul of the authorities in my very first issue. A fullpage frontispiece showed an English lord at a ringside table of a night club. A couple on the floor was doing "the shimmy"—a sexy dance craze of the moment. The caption had somebody asking the lord what he thought of the exhibition. "All I can sye," replied the lord, "is that I 'opes 'e marries the gal." President Nicholas Murray Butler took time out from busy life to explain to me (1) that English lords rarely spoke with cockney accents, and (2) that if succeeding issues of Jester contained any more questionable stories, I'd be out on my ear even faster than my predecessor.

This was a pretty sobering experience, and I drifted into the more serious side of the publishing business for many years—until 1942, to be precise, when the obvious need for material to make people laugh induced me to make a collection that ultimately appeared as THE Pocket BOOK OF WAR HUMOR. That was followed by THE Pocket BOOK OF CARTOONS, TRY AND STOP ME, and now LAUGHING STOCK. As Wolcott Gibbs once wrote about Harry Luce, "Where it all will end, knows God."

The majority of the stories in this book are neither as old as Joe Miller nor as new as penicillin. A lot of them were in general circulation before most of the people who will read them here were born—but good jokes, like good wines, mellow with age, and as so many wits have truthfully insisted, "There is no such thing as a really old joke. If *you* never heard it before, it's new." Most so-called "new stories" are simply dressed up versions of chestnuts anyhow. What Abe Lincoln used to tell Thaddeus Stevens now passes as conversation between Harry Truman and Jimmy Byrnes. Jet-propelled planes are substituted for tandem bicycles, psychoanalysts for village medicos, G-strings for bus-

(vi)

tles—and presto, a tale from "Traveling Through Arkansas" (published in the 1850's) becomes a new gag, claimed by three comedians and four Broadway columnists. If you are honest with yourself, you will admit that you too have been known to fall prey to that silly habit of claiming other people's jokes as your own. Jones tells you a story on the 8:8 that makes you laugh. When you arrive at the office you retell it to Johnson. Fifteen minutes later you overhear Johnson telling it to a friend over the telephone. With what fine rage you dash into Johnson's office and snarl "Hey! What's the idea of telling *my* story without giving me credit?" It's the ham in us—a universal trait, if slightly more pronounced in women than men. This is not an entirely unprejudiced estimate.

Many of the newer anecdotes in this book were sent to me by total strangers, and appeared first in my weekly Trade Winds column in the *Saturday Review of Literature*. These contributors commented in a superior sort of way about the antiquity of stories somebody else had submitted the week before, and ended by retailing a few choice samples of their own. This enchanting and labor-saving custom I have encouraged as vigorously as possible.

I have tried to scatter my own favorites throughout the book, rather than follow the time-honored custom of putting all the good apples at the top of the barrel. I have tried also to avoid giving offense to the most sensitive reader. This collection, like all others, has its full quota of Irish, Scotch, Jewish, Negro, and Cockney yarns, but every one of them, I think, plays up humorous qualities of the races involved without holding them up to ridicule or derision. Taciturn farmers and their beautiful daughters, salesmen, people of the theatre, inebriates, and all the rest of the inevitable and exaggerated characters people the volume. The average, everyday citizen is the backbone of the nation, but slim pickings for a joke book. He is supposed to buy it—not star in it!

Finally, this is a collection for reasonably adult and intelligent readers. I believe it normal and healthy to laugh at certain universal aspects of the S-E-X problem without leers or obscene whisperings. The vast popularity of the humor of Peter Arno, H. Allen Smith, Whitney Darrow, Jr., Earl Wilson, Richard Taylor, and the late Thorne Smith is evidence that a goodly percentage of American people agree with this theory.

A country's humor, like any other fashion, changes with the times. The reader of today, for instance, finds scant amusement in the writings of Bill Nye, Artemus Ward, and other celebrated wits of yesteryear. By the same token, the school of wise-crack, insult, and rapid-fire repartee, so popular today on the radio and elsewhere, will become passé in due course. I believe that the coming vogue in humor has already been forecast by the gentler, less sadistic, but soul-satisfying laughter evoked on the stage by such thumping successes as "Life with Father," "I Remember Mama," and "The Late George Apley." This is a development that most true devotees of humor will welcome with resounding cheers. The joke book of the future will bear little resemblance to this collection. My grandson will tell me (if I'm still kicking around at the time) "For Pete's sake, is *that* what people laughed at fifty years ago?" I only hope this book fares well enough to justify an answer of "Yes, you fresh young scalawag, *it certainly is!*"

The sections of this book headed "This Way to the Jokes," "A Handful of Definitions," and "Limerick Lane" appeared originally in "THE POCKET BOOK OF JOKES," which I edited, and which are reprinted in this more permanent format by permission of Pocket Books, Inc. I have taken advantage of the opportunity to add several stories here and there, and make a few necessary corrections. The section called "Last Laughs" is an exclusive feature of this volume. So are the inimitable drawings of Carl Rose.

I hope everybody will find a lot of stories in LAUGHING STOCK that he hasn't heard before—or, at least, not for so long that he's forgotten them!

BENNETT CERF

Contents

Contents

This Way to the Jokes

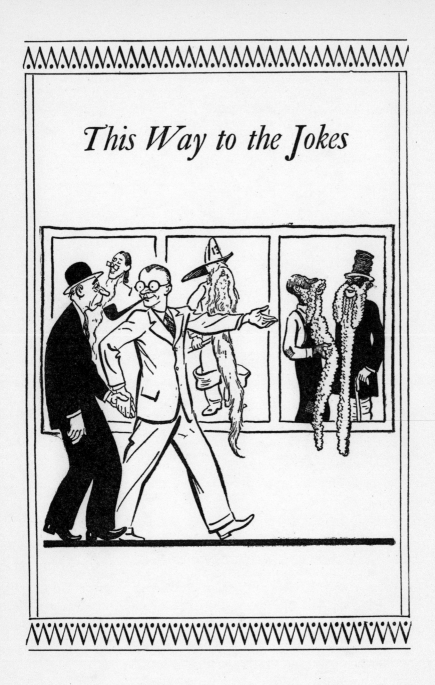

This Way to the Jokes

Two Passengers lolling in deck-chairs on the *Queen Mary* were boasting to each other of their prowess as salesmen.

"I'm from Schenectady," said one, "and you may not believe it, but the day before we sailed, I sold General Electric fifty thousand dollars' worth of cardboard boxes."

"What's that?" deprecated the other. "Nothing! I'll tell you about me. I run a clothing store in Glens Falls. The day before we sailed, a woman came in to buy a suit to bury her husband in—and I sold her an extra pair of pants."

»»*««

A famous maestro had a tough time deciding whether to marry a very beautiful but stupid girl or a rather painful looking creature who was blessed with a magnificent voice. Art triumphed. He married the soprano. The morning after their nuptials, he woke up, took one look at his bride, nudged her and shrieked, "For God's sake, SING."

»»*««

A race track habitué told his wife "The darndest thing happened to me at Jamaica this afternoon. I was bending down to tie my shoe-lace and some near-sighted goon strapped a saddle on me."

LAUGHING STOCK

"What did you do?" asked the wife.

"What the hell could I do?" complained the husband. "I came in third."

»»✳««

BETTY GRABLE entertained a five-year-old niece for a Hollywood week-end. She was in the tub bathing when the little girl entered the bathroom and asked if she could climb into the tub with her. "Come ahead," said Betty, and then noticed that the little girl was staring very intently at her.

"What's the matter?" she asked.

"I am wondering," said the niece, "why it is that I am so plain and you're so fancy."

»»✳««

"I'LL MAKE a new sport coat for you," agreed an overworked tailor, "but it won't be ready for thirty days." "Thirty days!" protested the customer. "Why, the Lord created the entire world in six days." "True," said the tailor. "And have you taken a good look at it lately?"

»»✳««

THE PASTOR finished a forceful sermon on the Ten Commandments. One parishioner was crushed momentarily, but soon perked up. "Anyway," he told himself, "I have never made a graven image."

»»✳««

SENATOR BARKLEY of Kentucky tells the story about the race-track patron who charged up to the wicket three times to place heavy bets on Blue Bell in the fourth race. When he appeared at the window for a fourth time, an onlooker tapped him on the shoulder. "Brother," he said, "I reckon this ain't

(2)

any of my business, but if I was you, I wouldn't be risking all that money on Blue Bell. He ain't gonna win that fourth race."

"Says you," jeered the better. "How d'ya figure that out all by yourself?"

"Well, if you must know," responded the other. "I happen to own Blue Bell and I jes' know he ain't goin' to win that race."

The other reflected for a minute. "Mebbe so," he allowed, "but if that is a fact, all I can say is it is going to be a mighty slow race. I own the other four horses."

»»✳««

THE TEACHER was determined to increase the vocabulary of her graduating class. "Now, boys," she said, "you've all heard about the great Prince Machiavelli. Can anybody use his name in a sentence?"

Little Willie's hand was up in a flash. "My father," he declared proudly, "can Machiavelli good pair of pants for $10."

The class had scarcely recovered from this blow when the teacher asked for a sentence containing the word meretricious. Willie—in fact, we might almost call him irrepressible Willie—was right back on his feet with "I wish you a Meretricious and a Happy New Year."

»»✳««

WHEN TONY'S WIFE passed away, he was almost inconsolable. At the cemetery he almost collapsed with grief; in the carriage riding back to New York his whole frame shook with wild sobs. "Now, now, Tony," soothed his friend, "it really is not so bad. I know it is tough now, but in sixamonth

(3)

maybe you find another beautiful bambina and firsta thing you know you get married again."

Tony turned to him in a rage. "Sixa month!" he shouted. "What I gonna do *tonight?*"

»»＊««

LUIGI AND VINCENTE made a solemn pact that the one who died first would make every effort to make contact with the one left on earth. Luigi was the first to go, and for months Vincente waited in vain for a word or a sign.

One day, however, as he was walking down a side street, he heard a low "Vincente, my friend! It's Luigi." He peered frantically in every direction, but the only living thing in sight was a spindly, underfed horse, hitched to a dilapidated

(4)

ice-wagon. "Yeah," said the horse sadly, "It's me, Luigi! Live as long as you can, Vincente, for see what happens when you die! This pig Guiseppe who owns me beats me, starves me, and makes me lug this ice-wagon around sixteen hours a day!" "But, Luigi," protested Vincente, "you can talk. Why don't you raise hell with Guiseppe." "S-s-s-h," cautioned Luigi. "For God's sake, don't let him know I can talk. He'll have me hollering 'Ice!' "

»» * ««

THE GOLF MATCH to end all golf matches was played up in Heaven by St. Peter and St. Paul. St. Peter had the honor on the first tee and promptly made a hole in one. St. Paul, undaunted, repeated the performance. St. Peter marked the scores down dutifully on his card, then remarked, "What do you say, Paul? Let's cut out the miracles and get down to business."

»» * ««

GELBER FROM CHICAGO and Greenbaum from Mt. Vernon met at Miami Beach and became fast friends in the course of a fortnight. On the train north to New York, Greenbaum insisted that his new friend spend a week-end with him at his home in Mt. Vernon before returning to Chicago. They had a fine time together, lots of good food and drinks, but when Monday morning came, Gelber was amazed to find a bill for $40 on his breakfast tray. "This is an outrage," he spluttered. "You insisted on my coming up here with you for the week-end, and now you want to charge me for it."

"Certainly," said Greenbaum. "You didn't think I was going to give you all this for nothing?"

(5)

The argument waxed fast and furious. Finally Greenbaum said, "I tell you what we'll do. We'll let the rabbi here decide who is right in this argument. Gelber agreed and the case was duly presented to the local rabbi. That worthy listened very carefully and he finally said, "Gelber must pay the $40." The Chicagoan was furious, but abided by his word and handed Greenbaum two $20 bills.

"I wouldn't dream of taking this money," said Greenbaum.

"What's the idea?" said the puzzled friend.

"I just wanted to show you," said Greenbaum, "what a terrible rabbi we've got here in Mt. Vernon."

»»*««

"PAPA," said the doting mother, "Robert's teacher says he ought to have an encyclopedia."

"Encyclopedia, my eye," grumbled the father. "Let him walk to school like I did."

»»*««

A CASTING DIRECTOR of a big Hollywood studio was interrupted by his secretary, who said, "There is a man outside who insists upon seeing you immediately."

"What does he do?" said the casting director.

"He tells me," said the secretary, "that he specializes in sticking his right arm into the lion's cage in big jungle pictures."

"That sounds interesting," said the director. "What does he call himself?"

"Lefty," said the secretary.

(6)

A TRAVELING SALESMAN, spending a night at an upstate hotel, ordered his dinner and then prepared to read his evening newspaper. The waitress interrupted. "You haven't ordered any of our potato soup," she chided.

"I don't like potato soup," said the traveler.

"Oh, but you must take some here," she insisted. "We are famous all over the state for our potato soup."

"I tell you I don't want any potato soup," he said testily, and turned away.

The waitress bit her lip and served his dinner in an aggrieved silence. Late that night the man who occupied the next room to the traveler had a violent attack of indigestion. His wife, who had much experience with this sort of thing, rushed down to the lobby and sought out the hotel physician. "Please go up to my husband's room," she begged, "and treat him. A high colonic always cures him. He'll fight like the devil against it, but if you simply insist, he will be completely cured in an hour."

The doctor made a slight mistake in rooms, with the result that the poor traveling salesman, despite his earnest protests and his shrieks of anguish, got the treatment that was intended for the man next door.

Two weeks later our hero met an old friend who announced his intention of spending a night at the hotel where the preceding events took place. "It's a fine hotel," admitted the traveler, "but let me give you a piece of advice. When they try to sell you potato soup, take it right with the dinner. They are bound to give it to you in one form or another."

A MADISON AVENUE BUS was unusually crowded one morning. A passenger sitting next to the window suddenly buried his head in his arms. The man next to him asked, "Are you sick? Can I do anything for you?"

"It's nothing like that," the other assured him. "I just hate to see old ladies standing."

»»*««

A MAN and his wife were sitting together in the living room one evening. The phone rang and the man answered. He said, on the phone, "How on earth should I know? Why don't you call the Coast Guard?" Then he hung up and returned to his newspaper.

The wife asked, "Who was that, dear?"

The husband said, "I haven't the faintest idea. Some silly jerk wanted to know if the coast was clear."

»»*««

A GUARD from the lunatic asylum rushed up to a farmer on the road and said, "I am looking for an escaped lunatic. Did he pass this way?"

The farmer puffed thoughtfully on his corn cob pipe and asked, "What does he look like?"

"He's very short," said the guard, "and he is very thin and he weighs about 350 pounds."

The farmer looked at him in amazement. "How can a man be short and thin and still weigh 350 pounds?" he asked.

"Don't act so surprised," said the guard angrily. "I told you he was crazy."

(8)

THE FAMOUS COMEDIAN, Harry Lauder, according to legend, was coming out of the stage door of the Palace Theatre one afternoon when a lady stepped into his path, shook a coin box under his nose, and reminded him "This is tag day for the hospital fund. Give till it hurts." "Madame," Mr. Lauder told her with a tremor in his voice, "the verra idea hurts."

»»*««

"Don't look now," whispered one lush into the ear of another lined up at the Malamute Saloon, "but theresh a fellow walkin' out of here this very minute with your hat and coat on."

»»*««

EVERY JOKE BOOK has to include at least one Chauncey Depew story, if only to keep its franchise. Well, Depew once paused to watch some kids in a sand-lot baseball game. "What's the score, son?" he asked one of the participants. "It's 28 to 0 agin' us right now," said the kid. "My," said Depew. "Aren't you a bit discouraged?" "Discouraged nothing," was the answer. "We ain't been to bat yet."

»»*««

AN OLD CANNIBAL chief sat anxiously outside the hut of the tribal witch doctor. That worthy finally appeared with a happy smile on his face. "Chief Wampum," he declared, "you are the father of a bouncing eight-pound baby boy. Do you want to take him with you or will you eat him here?"

»»*««

TWO OTHER cannibals—darned if they didn't belong to the very same tribe!—were strolling aimlessly down the jungle Fifth Avenue. "Who was that lady I seen you with last

(9)

night?" asked the first cannibal.

"That was no lady," the other assured him. "That was my dinner."

»»*««

A FAMOUS tragedian's wife died at the ripe old age of 73. When her body was lowered into the grave, the tragedian broke down completely. "I didn't know your wife meant so much to you," said a friend later. "You certainly were crying your eyes out at the cemetery."

"That was nothing at all," the tragedian assured him. "Nothing at all. You should have caught me at the funeral parlor."

»»*««

TWENTY GENTLEMEN in dinner coats and black ties dined long and well at the "21" Club, not exactly famous for its modest tariffs. The moment came for picking up the bill. "This is on me," cried several men, without too much enthusiasm, but, to everybody's astonishment, the voice of Algernon McSwiggen rang out above the lot. "This is a famous anniversary in the history of the clan McSwiggen," he announced cheerily, "and it will be my great pleasure, gentlemen, to pay for the dinner and all the drinks you can consume in the next three and a half hours."

The next morning the front page of the New York *Times* carried a big, black headline: "SCOTCH VENTRILO-QUIST MURDERED."

»»*««

A YOUNG MOUSE announced his engagement at lunch one day. "Tonight," said an older friend, "will decide whether you're a man or a mouse. If you kiss her tonight, you're a man. If you're afraid to assert yourself and put off the happy day, you're just a mouse."

"I guess I must be just a rat," said the young mouse sadly. "I kissed her *last* night."

»»*««

OLD PROFESSOR MCKEON cleared his throat in the midst of an examination period and remarked gently, "Will some generous student who isn't copying from his text-book be kind enough to let me have the use of it for a few moments?"

»»*««

THE FAMOUS black-face team of Moran and Mack had a great routine built around Mack's experiences in running a farm for a summer. Right at the start he explained, "We bought 1000 pigs at seventy five cents apiece and fattened them up all summer."

"What did you sell them for in the fall?" asked Mack.

"Seventy five cents apiece," said Moran.

"You sold them for the same price you bought 'em for!" said Mack. "You can't make any money that way."

Moran nodded sadly. "We found that out," he said.

Moran also had a lot of horses at his farm. "Funny thing," he reported. "The white horses always ate more than the black horses."

"How do you explain that?" asked Mack.

"I don't know," said Moran, "unless it was because we had more white horses."

»»*««

AFTER TWENTY-NINE YEARS of wedded bliss, a man's wife passed away and the bereaved husband had her ashes put into a beautiful urn, which he placed directly above the fireplace in his living room. Heedless friends fell into the habit of flicking their cigar ashes into the urn. His brother from Chicago arrived some weeks later, glanced into the urn, and remarked with some surprise, "Say, your wife is gaining weight!"

»»*««

THREE VERY FANCY young gentlemen skipped into a corner gin mill. "Sarsaparilla," demanded the first one firmly. "Coca-cola," ordered the second. "Make mine milk," said the third. "I'm doing the driving."

»»*««

A MAN named Chester Weil was bothered by an exaggerated case of dandruff and finally determined to do something about it. In one day he consulted four different barbers. The first one poured green tonic on his head. The second one used red tonic. The third one used blue tonic. The fourth remedy was a bright purple. Three days later he told a friend, "My dandruff is gone, but it's turned into confetti."

»»*««

A PROFESSIONAL POLITICIAN made a fervid campaign speech in the Brownsville section of Brooklyn for Tobias Ginsberg, who was running for assemblyman. "For every letter in the alphabet," shouted the orator, "Ginsberg has a virtue." Then he started counting off on his fingers. "A: He is able. B: He is brave. C: He is courageous. D: he is daring. E: He is efficient. F: He is frank. G: He is great. H: He is honest. I: He is intelligent. . . ."

One of the spectators in the front row, who had long been a personal foe of Ginsberg's, had been listening to this catalogue in growing impatience. Now he could stand the strain no longer. He jumped to his feet, pushed the orator into the background, and cried: "I will finish this list, ladies and gentlemen. J: He is a jerk. K: He is a krook. L: He is a louse. M: He is a murderer. N: He is a no-good. O: He is onbearable. P: He is a punk. Q: He is queer. R: He is a rat. S: He stinks. T: He is a thief. U: He is undependable. V: He is a varmint. W: He is a waster. And X Y Z: He is a general all around son-of-a-b—."

»»*««

McNAUGHTON LOOKED rather dejected as he was taking off his ice skates. "What's the matter?" asked his friend.

"I've been trying," said McNaughton, "to make a fancy figure for two hours."

"What happened?" prompted the friend.

"She slapped me in the face," sighed McNaughton.

»»*««

SIGN in a Miami Beach restaurant: "If you are over eighty years old and accompanied by your parents, we will cash your check."

»»*««

A MAN and his wife both believed firmly in reincarnation and made a solemn pact that the first one who died would devote all his efforts to communicating with the one who was still alive. In due course the husband passed away. Six months later, the widow was overjoyed to hear his voice one night as

(13)

she sat drowsing over a newspaper. "Hello, how's tricks?" he said as calmly as though he had only left her ten minutes before to have a drink at the corner saloon.

"Darling!" she cried. "How are you?"

"Fine and dandy," he said, "and there's a cow in the next field that has the most beautiful blue eyes you ever saw."

The widow brushed this startling information aside. "Tell me all about yourself," she insisted. "Are you happy?"

"Sure, I'm happy," he said impatiently. "But let me tell you some more about that cow. It's sort of black and white and has the softest skin. . . ."

"Gracious me," said the exasperated widow. "Here I am, dying to know about the secrets of reincarnation, and you keep talking to me about a fool cow."

"Oh," said the dead husband, "I guess I forgot to tell you. I am now a bull in Montana."

»»✳««

FOUR VERY DEAF old ladies played bridge every Tuesday afternoon. A startled visitor heard the following bidding take place after one hand had been dealt: The first lady bid four spades. "Three hearts," declared the second. "Two diamonds," said the third. "Well," said the fourth, "if nobody else has a bid, I'll try one club."

»»✳««

A BROADWAY PLAYBOY had a closer shave than he bargained for in a local barber shop recently. His manicure girl was very beautiful and the playboy suggested dinner and a show that evening. "I don't think I ought to," said the girl demurely. "I am married."

(14)

"Ask your husband," suggested the playboy. "I'm sure he wouldn't mind."

"Ask him yourself," said the girl. "He's shaving you."

»»*««

MR. GLEASON was nonchalant enough when he opened the door, but his guests, who had dropped in unannounced to pay a friendly call, stepped back with some surprise. Mr.

Gleason was stark naked except for a high silk hat which was clamped down firmly on his head.

"Well," said the lady. "Do you always go around the house naked this way?"

"Sure," said Gleason. "Nobody ever comes to see me."

"But what's the idea of the high hat?" persisted the lady.

Explained Gleason: "There's always a chance that *somebody* will drop in."

»»✳««

MR. AND MRS. WILLIAMS' happy married life almost went on the rocks because of the presence in the household of old Uncle Ezra. For twelve long years he lived with the Williamses, always crotchety, always demanding, always the first one at the table at mealtimes. Finally, the old man caught double pneumonia and died. On the way back from the cemetery, Mr. Williams told his wife that he had a confession to make. "Darling," he said, "if I didn't love you so much, I don't think I ever could have stood having your Uncle Ezra in the house all that time."

His wife looked at him, aghast. "*My* Uncle Ezra!" she cried. "I thought he was *your* Uncle Ezra."

»»✳««

WEE WILLIE DEEGAN loved his game of golf, but one bright, sunny day his friends saw him sitting disconsolately in the club house, his clubs nowhere in sight. "Why aren't you out playing, Willie?" asked a friend.

"Ach, I nae can play agin," sighed Willie.

"Why not?" asked his friend.

"Ach," said Willie, "I lost me ball."

»»✳««

A FRENCH UNDERSECRETARY was invited to the silver wedding anniversary of a distinguished English bishop. "Silver

(16)

wedding?" he asked the bishop's nephew. "It is a ceremony which I do not quite grasp."

"My uncle and aunt," was the reply, "have lived together for twenty-five long years without being separated a single day."

"Ah!" said the Frenchman. "And now he marry her? *Magnifique!*"

»»*««

THE GOOD SHIP *Donald Porter* got firmly stuck in the ice north of Greenland one winter, and it looked as though all hands were doomed to starvation. When the last piece of dried fish had been doled out, the brave captain stepped forward. "My hearties," he declared, "I got you into this mess and it's only fair that I be the first to go. You can eat me for a fortnight." He took out his trusty blunderbuss, pressed it to his temple, and was about to shoot when the second mate, Harper, cried, "Stop! Not that, Captain. Don't blow your brains out, I beg you. That's my favorite dish."

»»*««

A FAMOUS South-American playboy once approached Jack Spooner, head waiter at the Stork Club, and asked, "Jack, what's the biggest tip you ever got?"

"One hundred bucks," replied Spooner promptly.

The playboy pulled $20 bills from his roll. "Next time," he said, "when anybody asks you who gave you the biggest tip, don't forget to tell him that it was I."

"I sure will," said Spooner, pocketing the bills hastily.

"By the way," said the playboy, "what's the name of the fellow who gave you the $100?"

"You, sir," said Spooner, and fled.

O'CONNOR HAD HEARD that his old friend Murphy had married for the second time, but he didn't meet the new bride until some months later, when he bumped into the newlyweds in the lobby of a big New York hotel. He was horrified to observe that the new Mrs. Murphy wore an obvious wig, had one glass eye, a wooden leg and a set of false teeth that rattled ominously every time she moved a muscle. Completely taken aback, he whispered in Murphy's ear, "What came over you, John, to marry an old battleaxe like that?"

"You can speak up, my boy," said Murphy cheerfully. "She's deaf too."

»»*««

ROSIE ENTERTAINED so many male visitors in the parlor and things were so quiet while they were in attendance that Rosie's Papa finally grew suspicious. One night he told his wife, "I've got a wonderful invention that will help us check up on Rosie. It's a television periscope. Just turn it on when Rosie is in the parlor with her fella tonight. If he holds her hand, there'll be a green light. If he kisses her, there'll be a purple light."

The contraption was set in place, the male visitor arrived, and Papa settled back for a nap. His wife awakened him by shaking him violently. "Come quick, Papa," she cried, "and see the pretty rainbow."

»»*««

A DRUNKEN GENTLEMAN reeled out of his hotel and stumbled into a taxicab that was standing at the curb. "I wanna go around thish park thirty-nine times," he informed the cabby. The driver noted that the man was extremely well dressed.

(18)

He figured that his was not to reason why. He started driving around the park at a leisurely pace. After about a mile he was stopped by a red light. His fare banged on the window and demanded angrily, "Fashter, you idiot. Can't you see I'm in a terrible hurry?"

»»✳««

THEY TELL about another inebriated cavalier who boarded a taxi at 42nd Street and Broadway and, pointing to the revolving electric news sign on the Times Building, said, "Driver, jush follow that sign."

»»✳««

A LADY in Vermont wrote to the Department of Agriculture and asked for a little advice on the care of chickens. "Every morning for the past month," she said, "I have discovered three or four of my hens lying on their backs with their feet in the air. What's the cause of this?"

The Secretary of Agriculture spoke to three assistants who called in an Undersecretary of State and three or four Ambassadors who happened to be standing around. They all put their heads together and sent the lady a telegram. "Your hens," it read, "are dead."

»»✳««

"RASTUS," said a dusky belle, "You is goin' to have to jump out ob dat window cause sho' nuff dat am mah husband's footsteps ah heahs in de hall." "But Honey Chile," protested her visitor, "We is on de thirteenth floor." "Rastus," she said firmly, "You is gwine to jump nebedeless. Dis am no time for superstitions!"

(19)

A FUGITIVE SCIENTIST from a Boris Karloff horror picture dreamed up a serum that would bring inanimate objects to life. He surreptitiously tried it out on the statue of a great general in Central Park. Sure enough, the statue gave a quiver and a moment later the general, creaking a bit in the joints, climbed down from his pedestal. The scientist was overjoyed.

"I have given you life," he exulted. "Now tell me, General, what is the first thing you are going to do with it?"

"That's easy," rasped the general, ripping a gun from his holster. "I'm going to shoot about two million damn pigeons."

land Yard official fell into the spirit of the occasion and assured him that the entire London Police Force would be put on the job.

That night, as fate would have it, something went wrong with one of the gas pipes under Old Bond Street and fifty workmen were dispatched to locate the source of the trouble. They dug a ditch six feet wide straight across Old Bond Street, stopping traffic completely, of course, and exposing all the underground pipes to the open air. Early in the morning, the bereaved Scotchman appeared on the scene, took one look at the repair work in progress, and shook his head with reluctant approval. "I must say one thing for the rascals," he admitted. "They're thorough."

»»*««

THE PATROLMAN strolled up to a drunk who was leaning against a four-story building and remarked pleasantly, "An' phwhat is it yez think yez are doin' there, me buck?"

"Holding up the building," pronounced the drunk solemnly.

"Oh it is, is it," laughed the cop. "Well, yez had bitter come with me, me buck, and let the building fall down."

The drunk came with the cop, and the building fell down.

»»*««

ON THE MORNING of an important recital in London, a famous American violinist stopped in at a small Leicester Square shop and asked the girl for an E string. "Yes, sir," she replied dubiously, and disappeared for several minutes. When she returned, she had in her hand a box full of assorted pieces of cord, string, and old rubber bands. " 'Ere sir," she

(23)

said, "you pick hit yourself. I can't tell the bloody 'e strings from the she strings."

»»✻««

AN INDIGNANT LADY barged up to the host of a formal dinner party and said, "I will never enter your house again, sir. Your wife has just grossly insulted me."

"I'm sure there must be some mistake," soothed the host. "What did she say?"

"She said I was a woman of the streets," shrilled the woman.

"That's just her way," said the host. "I have been out of the Army for thirty years and she still calls me Colonel."

»»✻««

THE SENATE had just appropriated three billion dollars for post-offices, seven billion dollars for monuments, and fourteen billion dollars for roads leading nowhere, when there was a sudden commotion in one corner of the chamber. "Lock the doors, lock the doors," cried a gray-haired solon. "There's a dime gone from my pocket and nobody leaves this room until I find it."

»»✻««

MACLEISH SAW Mr. Ginsberg sitting alone on the first tee. "How about a twosome?" he suggested.

"What's the use of my playing with you?" said Mr. Ginsberg. "I have only played golf twice in my life and I wouldn't be able to give you much of a game."

"I am no good myself," declared MacLeish. "I just play for the exercise. Let's have a friendly little match for $50 on the side."

(24)

Three hours later Mr. Ginsberg sat slumped over a gin rickey in the locker room. "I shoulda known he was leading me on," he moaned. "He tells me he hardly ever plays the game, and then he does the eighteen holes in 69."

"How badly did he beat you?" asked a friend.

"One up," said Ginsberg.

»»*««

"You can't be sick here," said the admiral. "That's what you think," said the sailor.

»»*««

A rich but well-seasoned old maid in Philadelphia finally landed an eligible gent. She was dreadfully near-sighted, but, knowing how much stock he put in perfect physical health, was resolved to conceal this defect from him by hook or crook. One day she surreptitiously fastened a diamond stickpin into a tree, and later, seated with her swain on a bench two hundred yards away, exclaimed, "Look, darling! Isn't that a diamond sparkling in yonder oak tree?" I'm sure I couldn't see a diamond as far away as that," he marveled. "I'll get it for you," she said happily, and got up to retrieve it. Suddenly her house of cards collapsed. She tripped over a cow.

»»*««

Inmate No. 4622 of the alcoholic ward fingered his electric flashlight lovingly. "If I turn this beam straight up in the air," he said to inmate No. 4623, "I'll bet you a trillion dollars you can't climb up it."

"I'm wise to your tricks," sneered No. 4623. "I'd get half way up and you'd turn it off."

(25)

A VERY social-minded and serious lady was added to the board of a home for wayward and fallen girls. She made it her business to speak to each of the inmates personally, and

then came charging into her first directors' meeting. "It's high time," she declared, "that we begin trying to attract a better class of girls to this institution."

»»＊««

HAL SIMS, the bridge expert, got so tired of answering letters from strangers requesting elucidation on the fine points of the game that he vented his spleen on one enthusiast who asked him no fewer than six questions in a single letter by sending him a bill for professional services rendered. The agitated bridge player called up his lawyer and said, "Am I legally bound to pay this bill?"

"You are," said the lawyer. The next day the lawyer sent him a bill for legal advice.

»»✳««

"Doctor, doctor," called Mr. Schultz frantically, "come quick. You know my wife always sleeps with her mouth wide open undt just now a mouse ran down her throat."

"I'll be over in a few minutes," said the doctor. "Meanwhile, try waving a piece of cheese in front of her mouth and maybe the mouse will come out."

When the doctor reached the Schultz apartment, he found Mr. Schultz in his shirt sleeves waving a six-pound flounder frantically in front of the prostrate Mrs. Schultz's face. "What's the idea?" said the exasperated doctor. "I told you to wave a piece of cheese. Mice don't like flounders."

"I know, I know," gasped Mr. Schultz. "But we've got to get the cat out first."

»»✳««

"Thanks for the pie, lady," said the Chesterfieldian hobo. "It was particularly perfect." "Meaning what?" said the suspicious samaritan. "Meaning," said the hobo, "that if it was any better, you would never have given it to me, and if it was any worse, I could never have eaten it."

»»✳««

When Deacon Howe took the night boat to New York, the pastor asked him to order a Christmas sign to be tacked

(27)

over the door of the church. Howe promptly lost the note which gave the dimensions of the sign and the inscription that was to be printed thereon, so he wired the pastor, "Rush copy of motto and dimensions." A new lady clerk in the Western Union office got the reply and promptly fainted. It read, "Unto us a child is born. Eight feet long three feet wide."

»»✲««

A BOUNCER in a Bowery saloon threw a free-lunch moocher out on his ear four times running, but the undaunted victim kept staggering back for more. A customer watched the performance with unflagging interest, and finally tapped the bouncer on the shoulder. "Know why that bum keeps coming back in?" he observed. "You're putting too much backspin on him."

»»✲««

GEORGE JESSEL and three companions went down to Belmont one day to play the races. For the first race they selected Hotcha, and Jessel went to make the bet. When he rejoined his companions he said, "I met Satenstein. He says Hotcha stinks, so I bet on Whoozis." Hotcha finished first by six lengths.

In the second race, the syndicate selected Daisy Lou. Jessel reported, "I saw Satenstein again and he said Daisy Lou didn't have a prayer. He told me to bet on Chain Letter, so I did." Daisy Lou won this race at odds of 36 to 1. And so it went with all the remaining races on the card. Every time the four friends picked a winner, Satenstein met Jessel at the betting window and persuaded him to shift to a nag who finished out of the running. When the last race had been run, the four friends sat disconsolately tearing up all their tickets.

"I could stand some fresh roasted peanuts," said one of the men.

"I'll get them," said Jessel.

A few minutes later he was back with six bags of Crackerjacks. "I met Satenstein again," he explained.

»»✳««

THE SCOTCH chemistry professor was demonstrating the properties of various acids. "Watch carefully," he instructed. "I am going to drop this two shilling piece into this glass of acid. Will it dissolve?"

"No, sir," spoke up one student very promptly.

"No?" asked the demonstrator. "Perhaps you'll explain to the class why it won't dissolve."

"Because," came the answer, "if it would, you wouldn't drop it in."

»»✳««

HEYWOOD BROUN stepped off a New York-Chicago train one morning looking badly frayed. "I didn't sleep a wink on the train all night," he explained. "One of Singer's Midgets was in the upper above me and kept me awake all night pacing up and down."

»»✳««

IN ACCORDANCE with the time-honored curriculum of the State Penitentiary, "One-Eye" Shimkin spent part of his first morning at the prison barber shop. "New guy, ain't you?" hazarded the barber. "One-Eye" grunted assent. The barber set to work with his electric clipper, accompanying his art

(29)

with a running commentary on politics, baseball, sex, music, and the lamentable inefficiency of co-workers on either side of his chair. "By the way," he said at the end of his oration. "What you get sent up for, brother?" "One-Eye" Shimkin glared at him balefully with his good eye and answered, "The barber in de toid chair at Greco's talked too much, so one day I grabbed de razor outa his hand and cut de bum's troat wid it."

»»✳««

"WHAT'S THE CHARGE against this man?" asked the judge.

"Drunk and disorderly," reported the cop. "He was fighting with a taxi driver."

"Bring in the taxi driver," ordered the judge.

"That's it, your honor," said the cop. "There wasn't no taxi driver."

»»✳««

IN DARKEST BROOKLYN, a pupil reported to his nature teacher, "Dis morning I hoid a boid choiping."

"No, John," corrected the teacher. "You heard a bird chirping."

"Funny!" commented John. "I coulda swore it was a boid choiping!"

»»✳««

A WOMAN submitted a torrid love story to a confession magazine and waited impatiently for several weeks for a reply. When none was forthcoming she wired, "Please report on my story immediately as I have other irons in the fire." An answering wire—collect—read, "We have considered your story and advise you to put it with the other irons."

(30)

A RADIO COMIC regaled a dignified assemblage in a Park Avenue mansion with a number of jokes that were born at a men's smoker and should have been kept there. The fact that

nobody laughed did not deter the comic for a moment. Finally he ran down of his own momentum and asked the butler for a glass of water. The hostess added grimly, "And Charles, bring a cake of soap and a toothbrush with it."

»»✳««

AN EXCITED LADY burst into Mrs. Schnitzle's boudoir. "Your son, Mrs. Schnitzle!" she cried. "Your son!"

"What about my son?" demanded Mrs. Schnitzle.

"All the kids were playing a game, Mrs. Schnitzle, to see who could lean out of the window farthest. Your son won."

(3 1)

AN OLD New Hampshire storekeeper was breathing his last, and a sorrowful family surrounded his bed of pain. "Is Ma here?" he asked wearily. "Yes, Zeke," she replied. "And my oldest son?" "Yes." "And the other five boys?" "Yes." "And the four girls?" "Yes, Zeke." The failing patriarch struggled to a sitting position. "What's the big idea?" he shouted. "Who's tending the store?"

»»*««

ONE OF Lou Holtz's stories concerns a millionaire's madcap daughter who bought an automobile that could reach a speed of 175 miles an hour. The first morning that she had it, she went out to do a little innocent baiting of motorcycle cops. She had reached a speed of 90 miles an hour before she attracted one's attention. She waited until he had almost caught up with her and then raised her speed to 120. Again he managed to catch up with her. This time she stopped fooling and put her foot all the way down on the pedal. 175 miles an hour! The cop disappeared in a cloud of dust. This was not the young lady's idea of fun, so she turned around to find out what had happened to him. She found him wrecked in a ditch. "I almost got you that third time," he told her, "but you pulled away from me so fast that I thought my motorcycle had stopped, so I got off to see what happened."

»»*««

"BOJANGLES" ROBINSON knows a Harlem dowager who, after a lifetime of sin, decided to join the church. When the deacons plunged her into the icy river the first time she gasped, "I believe." After the second dunking she chattered, "I believe." A third time, gulping for air, she sputtered again,

"I believe." One of the elders asked her eagerly, "What do you believe, sister?"

She gave him a murderous look and declared, "I believe you stinkers are trying to drown me."

»»*««

A BIG SYNDICATE was about to launch a newspaper in a large city and offered a huge cash prize to the person who submitted the best name for it, along with a short essay on why that name should be used. One contestant suggested that the paper be called "The Truth." His reason: Every time anybody comes up to a newstand to buy a paper, the proprietor could say, "What do you want? 'The Truth' or 'The Tribune?' "

»»*««

A MODEST GIRL, asserts the *Army and Navy Journal*, never pursues a man. Nor, it continues, does a mousetrap pursue a mouse.

»»*««

A PULLMAN CONDUCTOR was going through the train one night when he found a red lantern hanging on one of the lower berths. He summoned the porter and said, "Why is that red lantern hanging on Lower Six, George?"

"Just look at rule No. 23," said George. "It says you should always hang up a red lantern when the rear end of a sleeper is exposed."

»»*««

THE POSTAL CLERK weighed McIntosh's letter and said, "It's too heavy. You'll have to put another stamp on it."

"What!" groaned McIntosh, "and make it even heavier!"

THE YOUNG LADY tapped the taxi-driver gently on the back. "Won't you put up your window, please?" she asked. "It's blowing papa's hair too much."

"How far can a little wind blow a man's hair?" sneered the driver.

"The last gust," she informed him, "blew it about three miles."

»»✶««

FIVE-YEAR-OLD CHRISTOPHER went to a party in a brand-new suit. When he came home, ragged holes had been cut into it with a pair of scissors. His mother gazed at him in consternation. "What did you do to your beautiful new suit?" she gasped.

"We decided to play grocery store," explained Christopher. "I was a piece of Swiss cheese."

»»✶««

MATT ROBERTS m.c.'d a dinner at which four speakers in succession grossly exceeded their time limits. The audience was writhing with discomfort. Roberts arose and said, "Before introducing the next speaker, I'd like to tell you of two skeletons imprisoned in a dark, musty closet. One of them finally grumbled, 'If we had any guts, we'd get out of here.' " Roberts says two vice-presidents were trampled in the stampede for the exits.

»»✶««

A PAIR of newlyweds stepped into their hotel elevator. "Hello, darling," murmured the pretty operator. There was

(34)

a chill silence all the way up, but when the couple reached their floor the bride exploded, "Who was that hussy?"

"Now don't you start anything," the groom said worriedly. "I'm going to have trouble enough explaining you to her tomorrow."

»»✳««

FOR MANY YEARS Mr. Brown had a little shop of his own in New York where he did all the work himself; only rarely did he venture out into the big world of business, and he met very few people. Suddenly, his business boomed, buyers were in and out of his factory all day long, and quite soon it became necessary for him to make trips all over the country. En route, he met more people than he ever dreamed existed, and he began to have trouble remembering faces.

After about a year, he bumped into a man on Broadway who seemed very familiar. "I know you from some place," said Brown. "Let me see. Oh, yes, I met you in the Royal Palms at Miami Beach."

The man said no, he had never been in Miami Beach.

"Of course, of course," said Brown. "Now I remember. You sat next to me at the Belmont Race Track."

"No, I never go to the races."

"Don't tell me. Let me see. . . . Why, certainly, we played gin rummy together all the way to Los Angeles last winter on the Super Chief."

"No, no," said the man. "Stop guessing, will you? I'm your brother Joe. Come home."

(35)

A Scotsman leaned against a mid-town bar holding his stomach and moaning piteously. "Sick?" asked a sympathetic stranger who stood next to him.

"Verra, verra sick," said the Scotsman. "I am afraid I've got yoors."

"What's 'yoors'?" asked the stranger.

The Scotsman brightened immediately. "Make it a scotch and soda," he said.

»»*««

Old Joe Slocum didn't know anybody was watching him fish until he heard a man's voice over his shoulder asking, "Catch anything, bub?"

'Catch anything?" said Joe. "Forty brook trout, that's all!"

"I guess you don't know who I am," continued the voice. "I'm the fishing warden around here, and you're breaking exactly six laws."

Joe was equal to the emergency. "I guess you don't know who I am either," he said. "I am the biggest durn liar in eight states."

»»*««

A harrassed guide had been trying to find something on the whole continent of Europe with which he could really impress a brazen, intolerant American tourist. In despair he played his last card—the magnificent view of the Alps from the Lausanne in Switzerland. "Isn't it the most beautiful view you've ever seen?" hazarded the guide.

"Oh, I don't know," said the American. "Take away your lakes and your mountains, and whaddaya got?"

(36)

AN INEBRIATED GENT with a very red, very bulbous proboscis, stumbled into a bar and ordered a double martini. Then he very carefully opened his coat and poured the drink into his left vest pocket. "Give me another double martini," he ordered. This drink too he poured into his vest pocket. When he repeated this procedure for a third time, the puzzled bartender demanded, "Hey, what's the idea of taking my

perfectly good martinis and pouring them into your pocket?"

The customer banged his fist on the bar and said, "Look here, fella. I pay my perfectly good money for those martinis and I want you to distinctly understand that what I do with them is none of your blankety-blank business."

At this point, a little mouse popped his head out of the customer's right-hand vest pocket and squeaked, "That goes for your cat too."

(37)

"WHEN," said the publisher to the poet, "did they open up that sidewalk cafe I saw you in last night?"

"That wasn't a sidewalk cafe," said the poet sadly. "That was my furniture."

»»*««

THE BOSS returned in a very good humor from lunch and called the whole staff in to listen to a couple of jokes he had picked up. Everybody but one girl in the corner laughed uproariously. "What's the matter?" grumbled the boss. "Haven't you got a sense of humor?"

"I don't have to laugh," said the girl. "I'm leaving Friday anyhow."

»»*««

BARNEY GALLANT's night club once had a lady dancer who climaxed her act by leaning over backward and picking up her handkerchief with her teeth. For an encore she leaned over backward again and picked up her teeth.

»»*««

TWO TACITURN Maine farmers met each other every morning for twenty years in the village post-office without exchanging a single word. One day, Farmer Billings turned left when he exited instead of right. "Where ya goin'?" asked his startled neighbor. "None o' yer durn business," snapped Billings. "And I wouldn't tell yer that much if yer warn't an old friend."

»»*««

SOMEBODY ONCE GAVE Henny Youngman a free ticket for an Army-Notre Dame game at the Yankee Stadium. Young-

(38)

man says the usher climbed with him to a certain point, but then pulled back, saying, "You'll have to make the rest of the ascent alone. Any higher than this, I get nose bleed." Youngman finally reached his seat. Sometime later he nudged the man next to him. "Great game, isn't it?" he hazarded. "Whaddya mean, game?" was the answer. "I'm flying the mail to Pittsburgh."

»»✻««

"WHAT'S THE IDEA of stopping in the middle of Central Park?" came an indignant voice from the back of the cab.

"Didn't I hear the young lady holler 'Stop'?" said the taxi driver.

"Get on with it," said the voice. "She wasn't talking to you."

»»✻««

THE TRAFFIC MANAGER appeared in his office with seven or eight pieces of plaster pasted on his countenance. "I was getting a shave today," he explained, "and a fellow from the barber school took his final examination on my face. Boy, did he flunk!"

»»✻««

A FATHER of a new-born infant and his best friend staged a celebration that covered at least twelve saloons. Finally they staggered up to the hospital to inspect the new arrival.

"Sh'all right," his friend assured him. "I only weighed three pounds myself when I was born."

"Thash terrible," said the father. "Did you live?"

"I certainly did," said the friend. "You oughta shee me now."

(39)

THE MAN who boarded a taxicab at Grand Central Station was so obviously a hayseed that the unscrupulous driver saw a chance for a bonanza. "I want to go to the Biltmore Hotel," said the fare. The Biltmore, of course, is a short half block from Grand Central Station, but the driver elected to follow a course that took him all the way up Riverside Drive to Spuyten Duyvil, across to Mosholu Parkway in the Bronx, and back to the Biltmore Hotel by way of the Bowery. At the end of the ride, the meter read exactly $14.35. The hayseed's face flushed with anger. "You can't play me for a sucker, goldarn it," he yelled angrily. "I been driven to this hotel once before from Grand Central Station, and the last time the fare was only $12.60."

»»✳««

LENNIE THE LUG found it difficult to laugh away the body of his sweetheart that had been found in his flat, and even the gang's slick lawyer felt that the jig was up. In a last-minute attempt to evade the electric chair he managed to contact a shifty-looking juror and whispered, "There's 500 bucks in this for you if you get them to bring in a verdict of murder in the second degree."

The jury was out all night and finally filed into the box, and the foreman gave his verdict: Murder in the second degree. Lennie the Lug was sentenced to 133 years in the brig with a possible five off for good behavior. The lawyer paid off in a nearby saloon. "What took you so long?" he demanded.

"Don't think it was easy sailing," protested the juror. "The

(40)

other eleven guys all wanted to acquit him, but I managed to talk them out of it."

»»✳««

CHARLES FINNEY once wrote a wonderful book called *The Circus of Dr. Lao.* The good doctor was a wizard in his spare time and his sideshow included several mythological big shots. One of them was Medusa, and the customers were warned not to look her in the eye lest they be turned to stone. A lady skeptic from Iowa ignored the injunction one day and was promptly transformed as advertised. Her rueful husband started to drag her out of the tent when an attendant rushed up and bawled, "Hey, you can't take that statue out of here."

"That ain't no statue," the man replied angrily. "That's my wife."

»»✳««

A LITTLE fruit dealer had a partner who cheated him first out of his entire share in the business, and then made off with his buxom young wife. The enraged fruit dealer caught the erring couple in flagrante delicious. He shook his fist in his partner's face and cried, "Some day, by golly, you gonna go too far."

»»✳««

WHEN GYPSY ROSE LEE heard that her *G-String Murders* was going to be published in London, she wired her publishers, "Who is going to make the English translation?"

»»✳««

A MOTHER lost her young daughter in the week-end confusion at Penn Station. After a frantic search she finally located her in the midst of a group of nuns. The little girl and

(41)

the nuns seemed to be having a very good time. "I hope my daughter hasn't been giving you too much trouble," said the relieved parent.

"On the contrary," chuckled the Mother Superior. "Your little girl seems to have the notion that we are penguins."

»»*««

A FAMOUS efficiency expert died and was accorded a magnificent funeral. The pallbearers were carrying the casket down the steps of the church when suddenly the lid popped open and the deceased sat upright to explain, "If you'd put this casket on wheels, you could lay off four men."

»»*««

LOUIS BROMFIELD, celebrated Ohio farmer, was boasting of the rich soil of his native state. "It hasn't got a patch on Georgia soil," Nunnally Johnson assured him. "Georgia soil is so rich that when we throw corn to the chickens, they have to catch it on the fly or eat it off the stalk."

»»*««

SID PERELMAN created a heroine whose first name was Avid and who had a passion for keeping Pullman-car porters at a respectful distance. The train was nearing its destination one time when a porter appeared and said, "May I brush you off, madam?"

"You may not," replied Avid icily. "I will descend in the usual manner."

»»*««

A MAN from Miami and a man from Los Angeles were busy telling lies to each other one morning at a California market. The man from Miami pointed to a large watermelon and

(42)

said, "Is that California's idea of a decent-sized grapefruit?"

The Californian squinted his eyes at the watermelon and said, "Out here we can't even see fruit that size. It must be a raisin."

»»✳««

A LADY entered a butcher shop and said to the clerk, "Give me two pounds of kidleys."

"I take it that you mean kidneys," corrected the butcher.

The lady snapped back, "I said kidleys, diddle I?"

»»✳««

OBER CALLED over the fence to Haas. "Didn't you always tell me that your boxer's bark was worse than his bite?"

"I did," said Haas.

"Better not let him bark then," said Ober grimly. "He just bit me."

»»✳««

A TIMID little lady approached the trainmaster at Wappinger Junction and said, "What time does the train for the north go by?"

"3:30," said the trainmaster.

A few minutes later she asked, "What time does the train for the south go by?"

"4:17," said the trainmaster.

A third time she approached and demanded, "What time does the train for the east pass here?"

"Tonight at 8," he answered.

Once more she approached him. "And what time does the train for the west go by?"

"There won't be another train for the west until tomor-

(43)

row evening," said the trainmaster wearily.

The old lady's face brightened. "Come along, Willie," she cried to the little boy on the platform. "It's safe to cross the tracks now."

»»*««

MR. COLLINS took his wife and eight-year-old son out for a spin in his brand-new Buick convertible. He had an idea that in his enthusiasm he would exceed the speed limit, so he posted his son in the rumble seat and told him, "Sonny, if you see a man in a blue uniform on a motorcycle coming up from behind, be sure to warn Daddy."

Off they went, and the delighted Mr. Collins drove faster and faster. The speedometer had just registered "seventy" when the eight-year-old tapped his father on the shoulder. "Daddy," he reported, "that gentleman you were expecting has arrived."

»»*««

IT REMAINED for Mr. Ray Freiman to discover the most important difference between a newspaper and a radio: You can't wrap a herring in a radio.

Mr. Freiman also tells about a woman who went to a butcher shop to buy a chicken. The butcher asked, "Do you wanna pullet?" The woman answered, "No, I'll carry it."

»»*««

THE DAY Gottfried got in his first shipment of Hershey bars in six months he was so delighted that he went on a wild spree. He wasn't used to hard liquor and about 11 o'clock he felt very, very sleepy. In fact, he was still very sleepy when he woke up the next morning. His brother eyed him

(44)

coldly when he entered the shop, rather shaky on his pins.

"Don't look at me that way," said Gottfried. "Just because I am an hour late for the first time in five years, you don't have to get sore."

"An hour late isn't what I'm worrying about," said his brother. "But where were you Tuesday and Wednesday?"

»»✳««

THE PHILANTHROPIST had presented the insane asylum with a beautiful new swimming pool.

"And how do the inmates like it?" he asked the warden.

"They're crazy about it," was the answer. "We can't keep 'em out. They'll like it even better when we put water in it."

»»✳««

TWO MEN trudged down Seventh Avenue in the noonday sun.

"You heard about that fellow Billings in Cincinnati?" queried one. "In the diamond business last year he made seventy thousand dollars."

"You got a few things wrong with that story," said the other calmly. "In the first place, his name was Burley, not Billings. In the second place, it was Toledo, not Cincinnati. In the third place, he ain't in diamonds; he's in costume jewelry. And in the fourth place, he didn't make seventy thousand dollars. He lost it."

»»✳««

"WHAT THIS BUSINESS needs," Mr. Jones told the applicant for a job, "is a chief worrier—somebody to do the worrying instead of me. The job pays three hundred bucks a week. Want it?"

(45)

"Sure I do," said the applicant. "Who pays me the three hundred?"

"That," said Mr. Jones, "is your first worry."

»»✳««

FARMER DEWITT had been on a tear in the big city and was suffering from a terrific hangover when he stumbled out at five in the morning to milk the cow.

"You look terrible," said the cow bluntly. "Those circles under your eyes reach down to your knees."

"I know," said the farmer sadly. "And milking you is only the beginning of my troubles. I'll be slaving on this durn farm till seven this evening."

"Well," volunteered the cow. "I'll help all I can. You just hold tight and I'll jump up and down."

»»✳««

A CERTAIN traffic cop on Central Avenue was the bane of existence for Messrs. Lapidus and Susskind. Every morning he would stop their cars and bawl them out unmercifully for some minor or imaginary violation. Every lunchtime the two friends would work themselves into a fine state of indignation over his behavior.

One day Lapidus announced, "Well, I finally told off that low-life cop on Central Avenue this morning."

Susskind was deeply impressed. "You didn't!" he said wonderingly.

"Yah," said Lapidus. "I got so mad I hardly knew what I was saying. 'Who do you think you are?' I told him. A czar? A big boss? You seem to forget you ain't nothing but a servant of the people. You are put at this spot to prevent

(46)

accidents and direct traffic—not insult taxpayers and peace-loving citizens who are going about their own business.' "

"Wonderful! Wonderful!" breathed Susskind reverently. "What did the cop say?"

Lapidus sighed: "He gave me a ticket."

»»✳««

THE HOUSE-GUEST noticed that Johnny eyed his asparagus longingly, but made no move to eat it. "What's the matter?" asked the guest. "Don't you like asparagus?"

"I love it," Johnny assured him, "but I have to wait for Papa to eat off the green tips!"

»»✳««

"BUSINESS ETHICS," the stationer told his son, "is something you couldn't do without. Take today for instance. A man comes in and pays me a hundred-dollar bill to clear up his account. After he leaves, I find two bills stuck together. He has paid me two hundred instead of one. Here, my son, comes in the question of business ethics. Should I tell my partner or shouldn't I?"

»»✳««

IN THE BASEMENT of the most squalid tenement on the most squalid street of East Boston a little tailor slaved fifteen hours of every twenty-four. At that, he barely made both ends meet. He allowed himself a single indulgence. Out of each week's meagre income he put aside twenty-five cents. At the end of the year, he took the accumulated savings and blew them in on lottery tickets for the Irish Sweepstakes.

For fourteen long years he never heard another word in regard to the tickets he had bought regularly, but one night

there came a loud knocking on his door and two splendifer-
ous gentlemen strode into his shop, slapped him heartily on
the back, and told him he had won the grand prize of $250,-
000. The tailor jumped to his feet with a hoarse cry of tri-
umph. He locked up his shop and threw the key into the
Charles River. He bought himself a wardrobe fit for a king,
rented a suite of eighteen rooms at the Ritz, and soon was
supporting half the chorus girls and models in town. Night
after night he caroused until dawn, throwing his money
around like a drunken sailor. At the end of a year he had
squandered the entire $250,000. Furthermore, he had
wrecked his health. Disillusioned, ridden with fever and exhausted, he reopened his little tailor shop and resumed his old
ways, saving only the twenty-five cents a week which, from
force of habit, went into new tickets for the Irish Sweepstakes.

Two years later there came another knock on his door.
The same two magnificent gentlemen came into the room.
"This is the most amazing thing in the history of the Sweepstakes," exclaimed one. "You've landed another first prize,
you lucky dog."

The tailor staggered to his feet with a groan of dismay.
"My God," he said, "Do I have to go through all that again?"

»»✳««

LEWIS YOUNG was accepting congratulations on the birth of
a baby daughter. "It's a wonderful baby," he declared. "6.11
the doctor said."

One friend looked a little surprised. "Isn't that rather tall
for an infant?" he asked.

(48)

JIMMY DURANTE claims an uncle who can play two instruments at the same time. "With the left side of his mouth," says Jimmy, "he plays 'Life Is Just a Bowl of Cherries.' With

the right side he plays 'Don't Sit Under the Apple Tree.' And with the middle of his mouth he blows out the seeds."

»»*««

IT WAS Walter Winchell who declared that he always praised the first show of a new theatrical season. "Who am I," he asked, "to stone the first cast?"

(49)

A LITTLE BOY and girl, both between five and six, were busy playing house one afternoon. Suddenly the little girl tugged at her mother's skirts. "I am afraid we'll have to leave now," she said gravely. "My husband just wet his pants."

»»*««

A BRITISH JUDGE wriggled impatiently on the bench while a lanky, vulture-beaked barrister summed up for fully an hour and a half. Finally the judge dispatched a little note to the garrulous legal light. It read:

Patience Competition. Gold medal—me.

Honorable mention—Job.

The lawyer wound up his plea in a hurry.

»»*««

A PAINTER was wielding his brush on the ceiling of a high room. His pal called out to him, "Have you got a firm grip on that brush?"

The fellow working on the ceiling answered, "You're darn right I have."

His mate on the floor said, "Okay. Then I'll take the ladder away for a little while."

»»*««

AFTER TWELVE DAYS of unceasing rain it became obvious that the turbulent Missouri was about to overflow its banks. An experienced farmer whose homestead bordered the river, packed his twelve-year-old son up and sent him to his uncle in the next state, asking that he be taken care of until the situation righted itself. A few days later the farmer received a collect telegram that read, "Am returning your son immediately. Send along the flood."

(50)

THE WIFE of a man whose business took him out of town very frequently planned her home life to coincide very neatly with his itinerary. One evening, when she fondly believed him to be in Chicago, she was happily providing food and entertainment for his best friend. Suddenly the phone rang. She answered and muttered hoarsely to her companion, "The saints preserve us. My husband has come back to town." Her companion, a cautious fellow, made a dive for his hat and overcoat, but the wife hung up with a happy smile and told him not to bother. "It's quite all right," she said. "My husband just explained that he won't be home until very late tonight because he is out playing gin rummy with you."

»»*««

THE VILLAGE SKINFLINT, desperately ill, startled the local pastor by wheezing, "Help me get well, Pastor, and I'll give the new church fund twenty-five thousand dollars." He recovered, but refused to receive the pastor on numerous occasions. The churchman finally cornered him in the post-office, sternly reminded him, "You promised the church fund twenty-five thousand dollars if you recovered your health."

"I did?" said the skinflint in astonishment. "That'll give you a rough idea of how sick I was!"

»»*««

"How's THE FOOD at that hotel I sent you to?" Martin asked his mother over the phone.

"There was a man here yesterday who simply raved over it," she reported. "This morning the attendants came and took him back to the asylum."

(5 1)

A MAN gave his son a sound box on the ears in the day coach of a New Haven train one morning, and an outraged lady who sat behind him pointed her umbrella at him and said, "If you don't stop abusing that boy, I am going to make trouble for you."

The man gave a hollow, mirthless laugh. "Lady," he said, "my wife just ran away with the iceman. The bank foreclosed my mortgage yesterday. We are on the wrong train. My son has just told me that he swallowed the tickets. And *you're* going to make trouble for *me!*"

»»✳««

RAOUL WALLING had always talked a terrific game of golf. One day a few of his friends decided to put him to the acid test and invited him to play over a strange course with them. Raoul arrived in a beautiful costume with tassels on his stockings and nineteen clubs in his bag. On the first tee he took a careful stance and then proceeded to fan the air four times in succession. After the fourth whiff he mopped his brow and muttered, "This is the hardest course I ever played."

»»✳««

A NATIVE of Brooklyn was spending his first day on a dude ranch in Nevada. He came back to the blunkhouse with a handful of rattles from an enormous rattlesnake. A ranch hand turned pale when he saw them and said, "Holy smoke, where'd you get hold of those things?"

The Brooklynite couldn't understand the other's agitation; he explained, "I took them offen the biggest woim I ever seen!"

(52)

A DUTCH Treat Club quartette broke into an impromptu rendition of "When Irish Eyes Are Smiling." A guest burst into tears. "I didn't know you were Irish," said his host.

"I'm not," said the guest. "I'm a musician."

»»*««

MR. GOLDFARB entered his flat in a terrible condition. His clothing was torn, his nose was bloody, and a couple of front teeth were missing completely. "What happened?" cried Mrs. Goldfarb in alarm.

"It's that no good Irish janitor," explained Mr. Goldfarb. "He tried to tell me that he had made love to every woman in this entire building except one."

Mrs. Goldfarb paused a moment to consider. "Hmpf, I'll bet that's that stuck-up Mrs. Steinberg on the fifth floor."

»»*««

PAPA RABBIT noticed with some interest that his young son was looking uncommonly contented with life. "What makes Junior so happy?" he asked Mama Rabbit when they were alone.

"He had a great day in school," she explained. "He learned to multiply."

»»*««

A PATRON on the beach at Coney Island left his wife alone for a few minutes. When he came back, he saw a crowd of excited people gathered at the water's edge. "What's the matter?" he asked a cop. "They just pulled some dame out of the water," was the reply. The man investigated and found that the rescued party was his wife. "What are you doing to her?" he cried. "We're giving her artificial respiration," was the

(53)

answer. "Artificial, hell," screamed the man. "Give her the real thing. I'll pay for it."

»»✳«««

THREE MIGHTY business tycoons were lunching together at the exclusive Colony Restaurant in New York. When the check came, tycoon No. 1 grabbed it, saying, "Let me pay this, boys. I am in the 50% income-tax bracket, so really only half of the check will come out of my pocket."

Tycoon No. 2 snatched it out of his hands, saying, "I am in the 70% bracket, so only 30% will come out of my pocket."

It was tycoon No. 3, however, who won the argument— and the right to pay the check—by observing, "Wait a minute, boys. My firm is operating on a cost-plus basis with the Government, so I will really make four bucks on the lunch."

»»✳«««

MRS. STANISLOWSKY was 81 years old. All her life she had lived in a little Polish farmhouse—three or four miles from the Russian border. One day her son came to her waving a copy of *Izvestia*, the Moscow newspaper. "Mama," he cried, "they've just signed a new treaty and the land we live on now belongs to Russia. We are not Poles any more, Mama, we're Russians."

Old Mrs. Stanislowsky nodded her head approvingly. "Thank the good Lord for that," she said with infinite satisfaction. "I don't think I could have stood another one of those cold Polish winters."

»»✳«««

AFTER "PA" HAWKINS had been a guest of the Chambersburg

Palace Hotel for thirty years, an interior decorator came through town one day and persuaded the management to do the whole place over. In due course the alterations were completed.

"These here new trappings sure are elegant," conceded Hawkins a few weeks later, "but I must admit I miss that old spittoon in the corner."

"You always did." A room clerk pointed out.

»»*««

ACCORDING TO BROADWAY LEGEND, Miss Beatrice Lillie opened a new show one night in Boston. Her friend and Compatriot, Noel Coward, was in New York at the time and dashed off a congratulatory wire. As a joke he signed the wire "Mayor Fiorello La Guardia." The telegraph operator said, "We can't allow you to impersonate Mayor La Guardia in a wire over our system."

"All right, then," said the playwright, "sign it 'Noel Coward.' "

"You can't use that name, either," said the clerk, who probably came from Brooklyn.

"But I *am* Noel Coward," said the playwright testily, and produced an indentification card to prove it.

"In that case," said the telegraph clerk, "you can sign it 'Mayor La Guardia.' "

»»*««

AN AMERICAN JOCKEY was riding in a steeplechase in Italy. His horse failed to negotiate the water jump and fell right on top of him. "Get off'n me," panted the jockey. The horse ignored him. "Din't cha hear me tell you to get off'n me?"

(55)

persisted the jockey. The horse sneered at him and muttered "No spika da English."

»»✳««

THE WILSON HOUSEHOLD in Maplewood consisted of Papa, Mama, a daughter aged 10, a son aged 8, and an Airedale terrier named Paddy, whom both kids adored passionately. One day during school hours Paddy was run over by a truck and killed. Mrs. Wilson dreaded telling the children, but decided there was no use beating around the bush. When they came home from school that afternoon she called them into the study and said, "Children, I'm afraid I've got bad news for you. Paddy was killed this morning."

To her surprise, neither of the children batted an eyelash. They noted that she had nothing further to say, rose quietly, and left the room. A few minutes later she heard both of them laughing merrily and gave a silent prayer of thanks that the task had proved so easy. Suddenly, however, she heard a terrific wailing and the two kids burst into the room. "Our poor Paddy, our poor Paddy," the little boy sobbed wildly.

"But I told you about it as soon as you came home from school," said Mrs. Wilson. "I said that Paddy had been killed and you didn't seem to mind it at all."

The boy looked at her, griefstriken. "We thought you said Daddy," he wailed.

»»✳««

TWO MEN-ABOUT-TOWN were recalling the most embarrassing moments of their lives. "I'd say my most embarrassing moment," mused one, "was the time I entered a crematory by

(56)

mistake and by way of cheerful greeting, cried "what's cooking?' "

"That's nothing at all," said the other. "I let myself in once for a nudist dinner party. The butler didn't say a word while I took off every stitch of my clothing in the hall. Then I threw back my shoulders and bravely marched into the dining room. Six people seated at the table, fully dressed, gazed at me in astonishment. I was in the wrong house."

»»✻««

THE LATE Jim McNamara met *his* social Waterloo when he was house guest at the home of the famous Deems Taylor. In front of a whole roomful of people, Jim pointed to a framed photograph on the grand piano and said, "Deems, why do you keep a picture of that old battleaxe right where everybody can see it?"

"That old battleaxe," said Taylor coldly, "happens to be my grandmother."

There was a moment's deep silence, broken finally by McNamara's piteous plea, "Is there a revolver in the house?"

»»✻««

A GREAT Harvard psychiatrist was conducting a series of experiments with a chimpanzee. He told his colleagues, "With sufficient patience, I am convinced I can teach that chimp to do anything. This afternoon I am going to try to make him play tennis." He took the chimp into one of the Harvard squash courts, sat it in a corner while he strode onto the court armed with a tennis racket and ball. For twenty minutes he banged the ball against the walls of the court, running madly to retrieve it, tripping himself up a couple of times, and once bashing his forehead with the racket. The chimp watched without moving. Finally the exhausted psychiatrist put the racket and ball within easy reach of the chimp, left the court, and closed the door behind him. Then he kneeled on the ground and peered through the keyhole to watch developments. What do you think he saw through the keyhole? A beady little brown eye!

»»*««

JUST BEFORE one of Mischa Elman's violin recitals, a man burst into his dressing room and greeted him effusively. "We're related, Mr. Elman," he announced. "Your wife's aunt is married to the uncle of my ex-wife's first husband's present wife." Mr. Elman puzzled over this for a moment and then smiled with relief. "It's not so close," he decided, "that I have to give you a free ticket to the concert this evening."

»»*««

"AN' FER WHOT is that loafer Duffy in the hospital again?" demanded the foreman. "It's drunk he was again, I'm thinkin'." "Positively not, sir," came Duffy's friend to the rescue. "It's a slight miscalculation Duffy must've been makin'. He comes down the ladder just as careful as you please about five minutes after some scurvy blackguard took the damn ladder away."

»»*««

"WALLIS," said Mrs. Howe firmly. "Willie is now eleven years old and it is high time that you told him about the bees and the flowers."

"Aw gee," said Howe, "I can't go through that song and dance."

(58)

"You'll have to," insisted Mrs. Howe, "or Lord knows what trouble he'll be getting himself into."

The reluctant father closeted himself with his bright-eyed young son. "Willie," he said slowly, "I guess you're old enough by this time to know how babies come, aren't you?"

"Why, of course, Pop," said Willie. "I have known all about that for years."

"Thank heaven," sighed Mr. Howe with relief. "Well, Willie, it is exactly the same with the bees and the flowers."

»»✳««

THREE TORTOISES were gathered in an English pub—a mature tortoise of about 200 years, a middle-aged tortoise of about 120, and an infant tortoise, who had barely turned 45. "Shucks" said the oldest tortoise suddenly. "I left my hat at that last pub we visited."

"I'll get it for you," volunteered Junior.

The two older tortoises resumed their conversation. Two weeks later they had scarcely shifted their positions at the pub bar. Tortoise Senior suddenly said, "Say, I wonder where that baby tortoise is. I bet he never got my hat."

"You can't depend on that child," agreed his companion. "He certainly ought to be back by this time."

Just then the voice of the baby tortoise came from the next room. "I heard you," he said angrily, "just for that I'm not going."

»»✳««

A SOUTHERN PACIFIC express train sped along the edge of one of the biggest cattle ranches in Texas. The passenger gazed intently at the huge herds grazing near the right of

(59)

way. When the boundary line of the ranch was finally reached, he turned to the man who occupied the seat with him and said, "Quite a herd of cattle on that ranch. I counted 11,422 head."

The man next to him gazed at him in astonishment. "That beats the Dutch," he announced. "I happen to be the owner of that ranch and I know for a certainty that I own exactly 11,422 head of cattle. How on earth did you manage to count them from a train that was going sixty miles an hour?"

"Oh, it's easy enough, if you know the system," said the mathematician. "I just count their legs and divide by four."

»»*««

MAMIE WAS POLISHING her nails behind the notions counter when a red-faced man in a loud checked suit swaggered over, almost knocked her down with a slap on the back, and demanded, "Hi, toots. Where can a guy go to wash his mitts?"

Mamie drew herself up haughtily. "There's a door down the end of this aisle," she said, "marked 'Gentlemen', but don't mind that. Go right in."

»»*««

A CUSTOMER who wore a tight-fitting coat with a ratty-looking fur collar stamped into a village A & P and told the startled clerk, "I would like to buy your entire stock of eggs, tomatoes, and over-ripe fruit."

"Gee willikins," said the clerk, "you must be going to see that old ham play *Julius Ceasar* at the Opera House tonight."

"I," said the customer, "am the old ham."

»»*««

AN AMERICAN SOLDIER was riding alongside a driver in the

front seat of a lorry in Southern England. He noticed that the driver had a big bag of powder at his feet and that every few moments he scattered some of his powder to the winds behind him. "What's the idea of the powder?" asked the American.

"It's lion powder," explained the driver.

"Lion powder?" repeated the American. "What is it supposed to do?"

"It keeps the lions away," said the driver.

The American pondered over this for a few moments, and then said, "Hey, I didn't know there were any lions in Sussex."

"There aren't," explained the driver, "and a bloody good thing too. The powder hain't no good."

»»*««

JAMIE HAMILTON reports from England that two young ladies were dining together at Lyon's—the English equivalent of Childs. One of them asked, "Is your boy friend a freethinker?"

The other replied, "Bles me, 'e 'ardly ever thinks of hanything helse."

»»*««

AN ARDENT ADMIRER of the stories of Ernest Hemingway was so inspired by that master's description of a lion hunt in Africa (see "The Short and Happy Life of Francis Macomber") that he decided to stage a similar safari himself. His wife said "Not without me," and his wife's mother also declared herself in on the party.

You have to have that background to understand the scene

that eventuated about six months later. The huntsman and his wife awakened in a jungle glade vaguely conscious of the fact that something was missing. The something, it developed, was Mama. They searched for her for about an hour—the wife avidly and the husband perfunctorily. Suddenly they found her cowering in a clearing with an enormous lion roaring at her ten feet away, crouched for a spring. "My God, Henry," shrilled the wife, "what will we do?"

"Nothing," said the husband promptly. "The lion got himself into that fix. Now let him get out of it."

»»*««

A MAN rushed into a corner drugstore and demanded a quick cure for a serious case of hiccoughs. The druggist promptly picked up a bottle and cracked it over the man's head. Down he went with a groan. "What did you do that for?" he moaned.

The druggist smiled proudly. "You haven't got your hiccoughs any more, have you?" he gloated.

"It wasn't for me," gasped the man. "I needed it for my wife. She is sitting in the car outside."

»»*««

A GROCER once told Bert Savoy that a bucketful of beans would cost him $10. "$10," exclaimed Savoy.

"Yes, sir," said the grocer firmly. "Them's high strung beans."

The same grocer then added pleasantly, "How about a little rat poison today?"

"Nothing doing," said Savoy. "Those rats will eat just what we do."

(62)

I THINK it was Bert Williams who first told the story of his hike along a hazardous mountain trail. "There I was mooching along on a path only four inches wide with a solid cliff on the left and a 6000-foot drop on the right. Suddenly I turns around and sees a lion chasing me. I begins to run like mad.

Then I comes to a turn in the path and what's in front of me but a great big tiger growling and lashing his tail."

"Heavens," said the straight man. "What did you do?"

"What could I do?" protested Mr. Williams. "The lion ate me."

(63)

ONE OF THE most famous sessions of the French Chamber of
Deputies involved a heated debate on whether or not French
women were to be given the right to vote. A Leftist deputy
wound up an impassioned address by crying: "It's a disgrace
that the wonderful women of France, famous throughout
the world for their chic, intelligence and beauty, should not
have equal rights with men. After all, in this modern world,
there is practically no difference between French men and
French women."

At this point a meek little deputy in back of the room
jumped to his feet and cried: "Vive la différence!"

»»*««

THREE STOUTISH LADIES were rocking gently one hot summer afternoon on the veranda of a modest hotel. "You should
have seen the jewelry I had last year," said the first. "My diamonds alone were worth $200,000. Unfortunately we had
to sell them all, since my Park Avenue doctor discovered I
have an allergy for jewelry."

"I assure you, ladies, I wouldn't be here at all," said the
second, "if I too didn't have an allergy. My husband and I
owned a ten-acre estate at Newport, but we had to sell it
when I found I had an allergy for salt water."

At this point the third lady fainted dead away. When she
came to, the others asked her what had happened. She explained, "I have an allergy for hot air."

»»*««

A MARRIED LADY and her boy friend were busily pursuing
l'amour when the lady's husband unexpectedly broke into
the apartment. "Well, well," said she disgustedly, "here comes

Mr. Big Mouth. By tomorrow the whole world will know about this."

»»✻««

A MAN hitched up the family nag and took his daughter for a drive. At a lonely stretch in the road, a masked bandit held them up. The man barely had time to whisper to his daughter, "Hide your diamond bracelet in your mouth."

The bandit took everything they had and drove off in their own gig, but he never found the bracelet. When he was out of sight, the father observed, "It's too bad we didn't bring your mama. We could have saved the horse and buggy."

»»✻««

THERE IS an interesting anecdote connected with the way Aaron Sussman, the great advertising magnate, got his original start in life. According to the legend, Sussman was sitting in a restaurant one day when he heard a sporty-looking gent at the next table declare, "My wife's favorite schnauzer died yesterday. I'd give $200 if I could find a good, thoroughbred schnauzer to replace it."

Sussman jumped to his feet and tapped the gentleman on a heavily padded shoulder. "I've got a thoroughbred schnauzer for sale," said Sussman, "but I won't sell it for a cent less than $250."

"That's mighty high for a schnauzer," said the stranger thoughtfully, "but I'd like to make my wife happy. It's a deal."

Sussman came back to his table with a satisfied smile on his lips. "Now," he told his companion, "all I've got to do is to find out what a schnauzer is."

(65)

THE HEADLINE honors on a certain vaudeville bill were shared by a comely blues singer and a man who exhibited a wonderful trained dog. The man, the girl, and the dog were taking a stroll between shows when the girl stopped and said, "Shucks, I'll have to go back. I have forgotten my cigarettes."

"That won't be necessary at all," said the man, "What kind do you smoke?"

"Luckies," said the girl.

The man stuck fifteen cents into the dog's jaws and said, "Jocko, run down to the corner and buy the lady a pack of Luckies. He'll be back with them in a minute," the man said confidently, but a quarter of an hour later there was no sign of the dog. Three blocks away they found the cause of the dog's delay. He had met a very handsome lady dog and nature was taking its course.

"So that's your wonderful trained dog," said the girl.

The man was mortified. "It is the first time in my life anything like this has happened," he said. "But I must add, in all fairness, that this is the first time he's had the money."

»»*««

A HARDENED New Jerseyite visited a Vermont farm for a vacation. The first night he was there, three hoot owls blew into his bedroom window. He seized his pillow and, after considerable thrashing about, succeeded in evicting the intruders. The next morning the innkeeper asked him if he had slept well. "Never had such a quiet night in my life," said the New Jerseyite. "I only saw three mosquitoes the whole night, and they were baby ones."

(66)

THERE LIVES one ham actor who is still burning at a Chicago critic's notice of his performance as King Richard the Third. "Mr. So-and-so played the king as if he were afraid someone else might play the ace."

»»*««

AN INDIGNANT DOWAGER, member of Boston's vast array of self-appointed guardians of other people's morals, burst into a police court. "Lieutenant," she snorted, "some disgusting urchins have chalked a lot of filthy four-letter words on the fence surrounding my house. And what's more, they haven't even spelled the words right!"

»»*««

IT WAS the eve of March 15th. "Chico," said Groucho Marx sadly, "the time has come to discuss our taxes."

"Datsa where my friend Ravelli lives," said Chico.

"No, no," corrected Graucho. "Not Texas. Taxes. The dollars we have to pay the government."

"Datsa what I said," insisted Chico. "Dallas, Texas."

»»*««

A CANNY POLITICIAN campaigning for re-election as sheriff, went from farm to farm drumming up votes. In one back yard he found a young girl milking a cow. He had just started talking to her when the mother stuck her head out of the back door and called, "Mary, who is that feller you're talkin' to?"

Mary explained that the visitor was a famous politician. "You come right into this house," commanded the mother. Then she added, "If that feller says he's a politician, you'd better bring the cow with you."

(67)

ON THE MORNING after their marriage, a bridegroom left his wife long enough to go down to the hotel lobby for a morning newspaper. When he came back, he was shocked to discover her nestled in the arms of a bell-boy. She looked at her husband coyly and remarked, "I bet you're going to think I'm an awful flirt."

»»*««

A QUAKER LADY noticed a man lounging idly in front of the hardware store across the way. Several men, she observed, stopped to talk to him and give him a little money. He seemed so cheered by these encounters that she impulsively put $2 in an envelope, wrote "Godspeed" on the outside, and threw it over to him. The next day the man rapped loudly at her door. "Here's your $58," he said cheerily. "Godspeed won at 28 to 1."

»»*««

CALLAGHAN was a very sick man indeed and his friends from the lodge took turns visiting him to keep up his spirits. The night O'Grady came, he was warned in advance that Callaghan was very low and he must be extremely careful to say nothing discouraging. O'Grady was doing beautifully and actually had Callaghan chuckling over a number of funny stories (by a strange coincidence several of them appear in earlier pages of this very volume). Suddenly, however, he stopped and began to shake his head. "What's the matter?" said Callaghan anxiously.

"I was just thinking," said O'Grady. "How in the name of the Holy Father are they going to get a coffin down the crooked stairs in this house?"

(68)

LITTLE JERRY came downstairs bellowing lustily. "What's the matter now?" said his mother.

"Papa was hanging pictures and just hit his thumb with a hammer," said Jerry.

"That's not so serious," soothed his mother. "A big man like you shouldn't cry at a trifle like that. Why didn't you just laugh?"

"I did," sobbed Jerry.

»»✳««

THE CHAIRMAN of the dinner, who tipped the scales at 220, mopped his brow and sank into his chair. The guest of honor jumped to his feet. "Gentlemen," he cried, "they tell a lovely fable in my country that when a baby is born, its guardian angel bestows upon it a kiss. If the kiss is on the brow, the child is destined to be an intellectual; on the eyes, it will be a great beauty; if it is on the fingers he will be a great artist. Now I am not in a position to tell you where the angel kissed our presiding officer, but you will admit that he makes a wonderful chairman."

»»✳««

A LITTLE whisk-broom asked his parents, "How did I get here?" His mother answered readily, "Your daddy and I swept together."

»»✳««

THAT INEVITABLY calls to mind the story of the man who found a rabbit reclining comfortably in the refrigerator. "What are *you* doing here?" demanded the man. "Doesn't it say 'Westinghouse' on the outside of this ice-box?" responded the rabbit. "Well, I'se Westing."

(69)

BELLOWS AND COMPANY, New York wine merchants, printed in their monthly house organ the following poem:

LONGEVITY

The horse and mule live thirty years
      And nothing know of wines and beers;
The goat and sheep at twenty die
      And never taste of Scotch or rye;
The cow drinks water by the ton
      And at eighteen is mostly done;
The dog at fifteen cashes in
      Without the aid of rum or gin;
The cat in milk and water soaks
      And then in twelve short years it croaks;
The modest, sober, bone-dry hen
      Lays eggs for nogs, then dies at ten.
All animals are strictly dry;
      They sinless live and swiftly die.
But sinful, ginful, rum-soaked men
      Survive for three-score years and ten.

A learned doctor perused this verse very carefully, and then penned the following reply:

Now, hark ye garglers of vermouth
      And listen to the sober truth.
The turtle, elephant and whale
      Eschew the use of beer and ale.
Yet you and I shall never know
      The age at which they're doomed to go.

The crocodile, that tearful beast,
Is ignorant of brewer's yeast,
But Cleopatra's childhood pet
For all we know is living yet.
The parrot, swan and other bird
Of ethanol has never heard,
Yet lives a century or more,
If anyone would keep the score.

This is no prohibition screed;
I drain the cup and smoke the weed,
And point a moral to this wheeze:
Pray, who would be as one of these?

»»✳«««

ONE OF THE most tempestuous actresses on the American stage is Miss Tallulah Bankhead. The author of a play in which she was rehearsing staggered away from one rehearsal and coined a phrase which threatens to become immortal in theatrical circles: "A day away from Tallullah is like a month in the country."

»»✳««

NUSSBAUM NOTICED the machine while he was waiting for a down-town express. "Your weight and your fortune for one cent," read the sign. "Shtussel-bussel," murmured Nussbaum. He stepped on to the scale and inserted a penny in the slot.

The card he got read, "Your name is Nussbaum and you weigh 148 pounds."

"It can't be," marveled Nussbaum. "It's a heccident."

He tried again. The second card read the same: "Your name is Nussbaum and you weigh 148 pounds."

(71)

A sandy-haired young Irishman was standing near by. "Please," called Nussbaum, "let me treat you to this machine. It's something unbelievable." The Irishman got on to the scale. His card read, "Your name is O'Flanerty and you weigh 126 pounds."

Nussbaum couldn't get over it. Once more he tried it himself. This time his card bore a longer message. "You damn fool," it read, "you've missed your train."

»» ✳ ««

A MOTORIST in Louisiana found the bridge over a stream washed away by a recent storm. A native sat whittling a stick by the side of the wreckage.

"How deep is this stream?" asked the motorist.

"Dunno."

"Think I can drive through it?"

"Sure thing. Why not?"

The emboldened motorist drove head-on into the stream. His car promptly sank out of sight, and he himself barely got out with his life.

"What do you mean by telling me I could drive through that stream?" he cried furiously. "Why, it's ten feet deep if it's an inch!"

The native scratched his head. "Can't understand it," he admitted. "The water's only up to *there* on the ducks!"

»» ✳ ««

THE WEATHER FORECASTER hadn't been right in three months, and his resignation caused little surprise. His alibi, however, pleased the city council. "I can't stand this town any longer," read his note. "The climate doesn't agree with me."

An American sailor bribed his way into a Turkish harem, was amazed to see a fat, bored eunuch playing a hose on a line-up of bewitching ladies. "A religious rite?" asked the

sailor. "Not at all," said the eunuch. "Orders. When one of them sizzles, I send her in to the sultan."

»»✳««

THE main course at the big civic dinner was baked ham with glazed sweet potatoes. Rabbi Jonas regretfully shook his

(73)

head when the platter was passed to him. "When," chided Father Kelly playfully, "are you going to forget that silly rule of yours and eat ham like the rest of us?"

"At your wedding reception, Father Kelly," said Rabbi Jonas promptly.

»»✳««

KLOPFEP FELL ASLEEP at the wheel, and the first thing he knew had driven smack into the living room of a roadside cottage. Embarrassed and humiliated, he climbed out of the car, and mumbled, "Can you tell me the way to Flemington?"

The farmer's wife said coldly, "Straight ahead through the curio cabinet, and bear left at the grand piano."

»»✳««

WHEN OLD DOC MCTAVISH retired, he gave his practice to his son, along with a final admonition. "Remember, bairn: when ye give patients a medicine, always instruct them to bring in a specimen."

"But Father, that's not always necessary, is it?"

"Of course not, bairn, but that's how ye git yer bottles back."

»»✳««

PROBABLY THE MOST famous and oft-repeated joke about Wall Street concerns the day a prosperous broker treated his friend to an automobile ride along the shore of Long Island Sound. "See that yacht over there?" he pointed. "That belongs to the great banker, J. P. Morgan. The one next to it belongs to Jules Bache." A little later he pointed out the yachts of other famous brokers: Mr. Hutton, Mr. Hornblower, Mr. Flagg, and a dozen more.

The frown on his friend's face grew deeper and deeper.

Finally he asked timidly, "Say, where are some of the customers' yachts?"

»»✳««

WHILE WE are on the subject of yachts, a man once said to J. P. Morgan, "I am thinking of buying a yacht myself. Tell me, what is the annual upkeep?"

"Any man," answered Mr. Morgan firmly, "who has to even ask about the annual upkeep can't afford one."

»»✳««

JOE FRISCO, the stuttering comedian, once received an expensive wrist watch from Charley Foy for valiant assistance in some benefit shows. "Take care of this," said Foy, who knew Frisco's penchant for pawning things. "I'll cherish it to my d-d-dying d-d-day," stuttered Joe. A few weeks later Foy spotted the watch on the wrist of his barber, who admitted he had bought it from Joe for $20. Foy bought it back, and gave it once more to Frisco. "You're a p-p-prince to do this, C-C-Charlie," said the comedian. "And if you f-f-find what I do with it this time, I insist that you k-k-keep the watch."

»»✳««

MRS. MORTIMER came home one evening arrayed in a new creation from a fancy Park Avenue milliner. She admitted to her husband that the hat had set her back $65. "You paid $65 for that monstrosity!" he cried. "It's a sin, that's what it is, a sin."

"Well, after all, my dear," said the wife complacently, admiring herself in the mirror, "the sin is on my head."

(75)

LITTLE MARY woke a candy-store proprietor from his afternoon nap and demanded, "A penny's worth of mixed candy." The proprietor threw her a vanilla and a chocolate caramel and grumbled, "Here, mix them yourself."

»»*««

THE PROSPEROUS and time-honored partnership of Jones & Johnson threatened to go on the rocks when Johnson fell madly in love with Jones's wife. Jones was very understanding about the whole thing, but finally told his partner, "This thing cannot go on any longer. The situation must be resolved one way or another."

"We've always been sporting men," said Johnson. "What do you think of the idea of playing one game of backgammon to see who gets the girl."

The husband thought this proposition over for a few moments and then agreed. "Let's play for a quarter a point on the side," he added, "just to make it interesting."

»»*««

DONALD OGDEN STEWART'S cabin-mate, crossing the Atlantic for the first time, woke him up the second morning out and anxiously inquired, "Do you think we're on time?" Stewart peered out of the porthole and solemnly declared, "No, we're about twenty minutes late." The great brain took this right in stride. "Wonder what caused the delay?" he mused. Stewart suggested, "Maybe the captain fell overboard."

»»*««

A LITTLE REFUGEE was trying to sell a crusty old isolationist a bill of goods. "I only buy from 100% Yankees," said the dubious prospect.

The refugee somehow managed to convince him that he indeed was a 100% Yankee, and sold him a fine order. As he was closing his sample case, however, he looked up and saw on the wall pictures of two distinguished-looking gentlemen —George Washington and Abraham Lincoln. "Fine-looking men," commented the refugee cheerily. "*Your partners?*"

»»*««

A CHAP had been complaining to an acquaintance in his office that he was having no luck finding attractive women to take out. His friend said, "I know just the thing for you. Drive up late one afternoon to Westport, and wait at the station for the train to pull in. The wives will be waiting to drive their husbands home, and there are always one or two husbands who miss the train. Ask one of the girls for a date, and she'll be so mad at her husband for failing to appear that she'll be glad to accept."

The man thought this a grand idea, and the very next day he started driving to Connecticut. He was quite excited and impatient, and when he got to Stamford, he thought, "Why should I go any farther? There's a station here, and I'll try my luck." So he waited for the train, and sure enough the men got off and drove away with their wives, and one beautiful girl was left over. He walked over to her and asked her to have dinner with him, and she accepted at once. They dined and wined and danced, and went back to her house for another drink or two. Just as matters were approaching a natural conclusion, the husband entered unexpectedly, and started screaming vituperations at his wife. Suddenly his attention was riveted on the man who was trying unsuccess-

(77)

fully to slide out of the back door. "So it's you, you rat," he bellowed. "I told you *Westport,* not Stamford."

»»*««

GOVERNOR HUNT of Wyoming tells this story on himself. He visited the State Penitentiary one day, and when the prisoners assembled for the evening meal, the warden unexpectedly asked him to make a few remarks. Without thinking he began, "Fellow citizens." Their smiles reminded him that all of them had lost their citizenship when convicted. He tried again. "Fellow convicts." This was worse. As a last resort, he explained hastily, "Well, men, I don't know what to call you, but I am certainly glad to see so many of you here."

»»*««

OLD MAN McRAE of the Purchase Fire Department was telling some of the young sprigs around the fire house of his exploits in the Gay Nineties. "I will never forget," he chuckled as he chewed an enormous wad of cut-plug tobacco, "the time we seen a woman on the roof of a ten-story building that was burning like anything over in White Plains. 'Jump,' we yelled. 'I don't wanna,' she yelled back. 'Go ahead and jump, lady,' I hollored. 'We got a net down here to catch you in.' 'Okay,' she said. 'Here I come,' and she jumped. We just laughed and laughed and laughed. *We didn't have no net.*"

»»*««

THE LIEUTENANT on duty at the 14th precinct station heard an excited lady's voice over the phone. "Send somebody right over," she shrilled. "There is an enormous gray animal in my garden pulling up cabbages with his tail."

"What's he doing with them?" asked the copper.

"If I told you," said the voice, "you'd never believe me."

(78)

A TAXI DRIVER ordered a steak in a downtown diner. He couldn't even make a dent in it with his knife and hollered, "Hey, this is horse meat."

"Sure, it's horse meat," said the chef. "Everybody is eating horse meat nowadays."

"That may be," said the taxi driver. "But the next time you serve it, why don't you take the harness of?"

»»*««

WHEN AN all-Texas regiment landed in North Africa, the captain is said to have warned them, "Remember, we got to humor the natives. If they say Africa is bigger than Texas, agree with them."

»»*««

A LOCAL Romeo's face appeared in the window of his beloved's bedroom. "Get a move on," he hollered, "and let's get this eloping business over with."

"Be quiet," cautioned Juliet. "Papa'll hear us and spoil all our plans."

"I wouldn't worry about that," said Romeo. "He's down on the ground holding the ladder."

»»*««

IN THE early days in Arizona when frontier justice was the rule, there was one two-fisted judge who ruled his court with an iron hand plus a pair of six-shooters. The only book in the whole town was an authentic first edition of a Sears Roebuck catalogue. The judge kept it on his desk and whenever it came time to give a sentence, he would consult its pages. One morning he opened the book at random, glanced at the open page, and shook a gnarled finger at a prisoner. "I fine you," he said, "$3.49."

(79)

The prisoner started to protest. "Shut up," whispered his lawyer. "You're the luckiest coot in town. Supposin' he had turned to 'pianos' instead of 'babies' dresses?"

»»✳««

A CERTAIN LADY who lived on Park Avenue loved birds and her husband was rich enough to indulge her every whim. For a birthday present he found her a parrot that spoke eleven languages and that cost him exactly $100 for each language. When he got home, he said, "What d'ya think of that wonderful bird I sent you?"

"It was elegant," she answered. "It's in the oven right now."

The husband's face turned purple. "In the oven?" he shouted. "Why, that bird could speak eleven languages."

The wife asked, "Then why didn't it say something?"

»»✳««

A JEEP rounded a corner on two wheels, knocked down a policeman and four pedestrians, overturned a fruit cart, and finally wrapped itself around a telegraph pole. A sweet young thing climbed out of the wreckage. "Yippee," she cried, "that's what I call a kiss."

»»✳««

"I PRESCRIBE absolute quiet for your husband," said the doctor. "Here's a sleeping powder." "When do I give it to him?" asked the wife. "You don't give it to him," said the doctor. "You take it yourself."

»»✳««

THE CADDY MASTER of a golf course attached to a summer vacation hotel felt that he was performing a good deed all

(80)

around when he introduced a young man who stuttered very badly to a female guest who suffered from the same complaint. The two took their drives from the first tee and, as they walked off down the fairway, the young man explained, "My name is P-P-P-Peter, but I am not a s-s-s-saint."

The girl answered, "Mine is Mary, but I'm not a v-v-v-very good player."

»»*««

TWO HUSBANDS whose wives went off for a summer vacation left them to keep house as best they might. One evening they purchased a four-pound sirloin steak. They left it on the kitchen table while they went into the dining room for a couple of cocktails. What with a few extra dividends, they were slightly rocky when they re-entered the kitchen, but not rocky enough to overlook the fact that their four-pound steak had disappeared. A frantic search proved unproductive, but then one of the men noticed that the cat was licking his whiskers with an uncommonly satisfied air. "I'll bet that cat ate our steak," he exclaimed. "One way to find out," said the other grimly. He seized the cat by the scruff of the neck and deposited it on the bathroom scales. Sure enough, it weighed exactly four pounds. "Well," he announced triumphantly, "there's our steak, all right. Now where's the cat?"

»»*««

"WHAT DO you do for a living?" asked the judge.

"I am night orderly at the hospital," said the prisoner.

"Thirty days for pan-handling," said the judge.

»»*««

THE MAYOR of a California town had just called the board of

(81)

aldermen to order, when a violent earthquake occurred. The mayor dove out of the nearest window, closely followed by the aldermen. The faithful secretary noted in the record, "Upon motion of the city hall, the meeting was unanimously adjourned."

»»*««

AN INDIGNANT DOWAGER once demanded of Dr. Gallup, the famous sampler of public opinion on practically everything, why she had never been questioned on any subject whatever. "Madam," soothed Gallup, "don't you realize that your mathematical chances of being interviewed are about equal to your chance of being struck by lightning?"

The lady answered, "I *have* been struck by lightning."

»»*««

QUENTIN REYNOLDS insists that a recent national poll was conducted for the sole purpose of determining why men get up in the middle of the night. Only 2.4%, it developed, really have to get up. 1.6% go prowling around the kitchen to find something to eat.

The other 96% get up to go home.

»»*««

SADIE's twelve-year-old son got a job during his summer vacation that paid $9 a week. "And, Mama," he promised, "all of it goes straight to you." When he handed her his first pay envelope, the contents added up to only $8.95. "Ah ha," said Sadie, "taking out goils already!"

»»*««

YES, SIR, it was those two famous Irishmen, Pat and Mike, walking down Third Avenue together. Pat dropped behind

(82)

for a moment; when he came back he was wiping his hands vigorously with a handkerchief. "If Oi catch the son-of-a-gun who spits like a quarter," he muttered darkly, "Oi'll break him in two."

»»✳««

A DRUNK in the Empire State Building stepped into an elevator shaft and dropped thirty stories to the basement. When he landed, he shook his fist and remarked, "I shaid up, not down."

»»✳««

GEORGE WHARTON PEPPER tells a poignant story of the days when Cal Coolidge was Vice-President. The Coolidges lived in the Willard Hotel in Washington. A fire alarm in the middle of the night brought every guest into the lobby, in a variety of negligees and fancy pajamas. Mr. Coolidge speedily surmised that there was no danger and started to trudge back to his room. "Nothing doing," said the fire marshal, "get back in that lobby."

"You are speaking to the Vice-President," said Coolidge with some dignity.

"Okay, then," said the marshal. "Go ahead."

A moment later he called suspiciously, "What are you Vice-President of?"

"The United States," said Coolidge.

"Come right back down here," ordered the marshal. "I thought you were Vice-President of the hotel."

»»✳««

"Do you know how to make anti-freeze, Mister?"

"Sure. Hide her pajamas."

(83)

MRS. MAULE thought that $4 was a very reasonable price for a thoroughbred police dog, so she clipped out the ad in the suburban newspaper that proclaimed this extraordinary bargain, wrote out a check, and ordered the dog to be shipped to her residence. A few days later the expressman deposited on her doorstep the mangiest-looking mongrel she had ever seen. In a rage she telephoned the man who had inserted the ad, and said, "What do you mean by calling that mutt a thoroughbred police dog?"

"He is just that," was the solemn reply. "Don't be deceived by his looks. He's in the Secret Service."

»» * ««

DIXON WECTER tells the story about a prominent rector of a New Haven Episcopal Church who was presented with a shiny new Packard. Driving down to Manhattan in his handsome new machine, the good Father found himself exhilarated and a little confused. Suddenly discovering that he was going in the wrong direction on a one-way street, he tried to extricate himself by making an illegal turn and then went past a red light. A burly policeman appeared and, with a bow, waved him to the curb. Leaning on the door, he said gently, "Father, I am afraid you are breaking about five traffic rules at once. Of course, it is okay by me, but I better warn you, Father, that the cop on the next beat is a Baptist."

»» * ««

A FAMOUS banker was being driven downtown. The car was suddenly sideswiped by a big truck and the chauffeur was badly injured. The chauffeur needed a blood transfusion on the spot and the banker, in a sudden fit of generosity, volun-

(84)

teered to supply the blood. The story, however, has an unhappy ending. The shock of ice water in the chauffeur's veins was so severe that he got double pneumonia and died the next morning.

»»*««

Squire Perkins had an ambitious son who went to New York to make his fortune. The breaks were against him, however, and he ended up as a bootblack in Grand Central Station. Squire Perkins continued to work his farm. Now the father makes hay while the son shines.

»»*««

"$200 for an electric ice-box! Too much! Good day," said the prospective client. The next morning he ordered the box over the phone for immediate delivery. "Might I ask, Mr. Mayes, what made you change your mind?"

"Certainly," said the client. "When I came home yesterday, my wife was leaning over the old ice-box, and I gave her a playful pat. Without looking up, she said, 'Fifteen pounds today, dear.' "

»»*««

The slightly over-rouged young lady summoned the headwaiter. "That's Clark Gable at the bar, isn't it?" he asked. He assured her that it was. "He's annoying me," she said. "Annoying you?" The headwaiter raised an eyebrow. "Why, he hasn't even looked at you!" "That," said the young lady, "is what's annoying me."

»»*««

"Christmas," explained a young radical, "is the time of year when bosses throw their dogs a bonus."

(85)

MAGGIE, the Foster's maid, had a perfectly infuriating habit of interrupting her mistress with petty household problems in the middle of bridge games for high stakes. One day her mistress threatened that if she ever interrupted again, she would be fired on the spot.

About two weeks later the cards had just been dealt for a hand when Maggie appeared in the doorway. The mistress saw her, but, as a test, ignored her completely while the hand was bid and carefully played. After the score had been entered, the mistress turned sweetly to Maggie and said, "I am glad you learned your lesson, Maggie. Now tell me what is on your mind."

"I just wanted to say," said Maggie, "that the house is on fire."

»»✻««

RAFFERTY'S COAL truck got stuck in the mud and Rafferty couldn't extricate it although he tipped the scales at a cool 260 pounds, and had been a strong-man in the Barnum & Bailey circus for nine years. He was standing by the truck cursing impotently when a lady walked by carrying a mangy little Pekinese dog. Rafferty's face lit with a sudden inspiration, and he asked the lady if he could have the use of the Peke for a few minutes. "What on earth for?" said the lady distastefully. "I want him to help me get this truck out of the mud," said Rafferty. "How can a little dog like this help a big loafer like you get a truck out of the mud?" asked the lady, definitely aghast. Rafferty explained, "I gotta whip."

»»✻««

A LADY in San Francisco was eating her lunch when the tele-

(86)

phone rang. Bedelia answered, giggled shrilly, said "Sure is," and hung up. A moment later the phone rang again—short, insistent jinglings of the bell. Again Bedelia answered, laughed even louder, called "Sure is," and hung up the receiver. The lady was puzzled. "What's going on there, Bedelia?" she asked.

"Strangest thing in the world," explained Bedelia. "Some fool person on that phone calls up just to say 'Long distance from New York.' So I says 'sure is' and hang up."

»»✳««

"I'D MARRY Pauline tomorrow," the young man told his friend, "if I could only make enough money to keep house for two."

"Why don't you go and live with her parents?" suggested the friend.

"That's out," said the young man. "They're living with *their* parents."

»»✳««

"MAMA," said little Linda, "do all fairy tales begin with 'once upon a time'?"

"No, darling," said Mama grimly. "Sometimes they begin, 'My love, I will be detained at the office pretty late tonight.'"

»»✳««

A SUCCESSFUL city business man took up farming as a sideline. After two years a friend asked him, "How are you doing with that poultry you put in?"

"My son is running it," said the business man, "and he seems to be doing okay. I bought the chickens for him, I pay for their feed, I buy the eggs from him, and he eats them."

(87)

The friend laughed. The business man was a little bit hurt. "I made $10,000 last year on the whole farm, however," he said.

"$10,000," repeated the friend incredulously.

"Yes, sir," said the business man firmly. "I only lost $22,000 this year. The first year I lost $32,000."

»»✳«««

AT THE HEIGHT of a terrific domestic crisis, a very indignant wife reminded her husband, "Don't forget that I come from an extremely aristocratic family."

"Come from, my eye," snarled her husband. "You brought the whole lot of them with you."

»»✳«««

THE TEACHER was classifying a new pupil. "Who gave us this beautiful school?" she asked.

"President Roosevelt," he replied.

"Who gave us our wonderful transcontinental roads?"

"President Roosevelt."

"Who makes the trees grow and the flowers blossom?"

"God," answered the pupil.

At this point an angry voice from the rear cried, "Throw that damn Republican out."

»»✳«««

YOU PROBABLY have heard of the magician who walked down Broadway and turned into a drugstore. Chances are he's the same fellow who thought Western Union was a cowboy's underwear.

»»✳«««

EZEKIEL HUBBARD was running for sheriff in a New Hampshire county and left no stone unturned in his quest for votes.

(88)

He went from farm to farm canvassing the electorate. Mrs. Rockwell saw him coming up the lane one afternoon and reached for a broom. "Get off my property, you good-for-nothing loafer," she cried.

"But, Mrs. Rockwell," remonstrated Ezekiel, "I have just come to ask if you will vote for me for sheriff."

"Sheriff," snorted Mrs. Rockwell. "You ought to be *in* the lockup, not running it. You're a scoundrel and your father was a scoundrel and your grandfather was a scoundrel. Get out of my sight before I take this broom to you."

Ezekiel considered discretion the better part of valor and departed. Before climbing back into his ancient Model T Ford, he pulled out his notebook and entered, after the name of Rockwell, one word: "Doubtful."

»»✳«««

IT HAPPENED that Goldfarb left New York for Chicago on the very day that Rifkind left Chicago for New York. Both men were aristocrats in ready-to-wear and would never have dreamed of traveling on anything but the Twentieth-Century.

The two crack trains reach Buffalo simultaneously, and Goldfarb and Rifkind met while strolling up and down the Buffalo platform. They became so engrossed in a business conversation that, without thinking, they both climbed aboard the eastbound train. A full hour later Goldfarb stopped short in the middle of an analysis of the button situation and said, "Rifkind, have you ever thought what a wonderful age this is we live in?" "How do you mean?" asked Rifkind, warily. "Well, take today for instance," pondered

Goldfarb. "Here I am going from New York to Chicago; you are going from Chicago to New York—*and we're on the same train.*"

»»*««

AN ENTERPRISING motor concern was staging a preview of post-war models. One visitor pointed to the most expensive model and inquired, "If I bought this car by installments, how long would it take me to pay for it?"

"That depends on how much you can afford to give each month," said the salesman, cautiously.

"I think I could promote $3 a month," figured the prospect.

"$3 a month!" echoed the salesman. "At that rate, it would take you a hundred years to pay up."

"So what?" said the young man. "It's worth it."

»»*««

"WHERE DID you stay in Atlantic City?" a merchant asked his partner after a long week-end.

"At the Benjamin Franklin," said his partner.

"The Benjamin Franklin? That ain't in Atlantic City! That's in Philadelphia!" ejaculated the merchant.

"Ah *hah,*" said the partner. "No *wonder* it was such a long walk to the beach!"

»»*««

ON THE MORNING of a World Series game an office boy braced his boss and started, "Sir, my grandmother . . ."

The boss caught him short. "Oh, come now, son, you don't think you are going to get away with that old chestnut about your grandmother having died."

"Oh, no," was the reply. "She's home on furlough."

(90)

A HOLLYWOOD DIRECTOR almost had apoplexy when an assistant trotted a two-headed man into his studio. "No, no, you idiot," he roared. "I said a tow-headed man."

"I THINK I will have a sardine sandwich," said Mr. Ekhammer to the waiter.

"Domestic or imported?" asked the waiter.

"What's the difference?" said Ekhammer.

"Only that the domestic one costs a quarter and the imported one costs thirty-five cents."

"You bring me the domestic one," said Ekhammer. "I'll be danged if I am going to pay boat fare to America for any sardines."

THE SUDDEN appearance of about fifty new anthologies in bookstores last year led one wit to remark, "If you steal one man's stuff, it's plagiarism. If you steal that of several men, it's research."

Dorothy Parker once defined anthologists as lazy fellows who liked to spend a quiet evening at home "raiding a good book."

»»*««

A FAT DOWAGER in a crowded Madison Avenue bus trod upon the foot of an irritable gent who was trying to read his newspaper. "Madam," he said coldly, "I will ask you to kindly get off my foot."

"Put your foot where it belongs," she replied sharply.

"Don't tempt me, Madam, don't tempt me," he murmured.

»»*««

CREDIT MR. BEADSLEY with good sportsmanship. When his store went bankrupt after two weeks of dismal business, he plastered a big sign on the window that read: "Opened by mistake."

»»*««

IN THE OZARKS, where whiskey flows like water, they have their own definition of intoxication. In a village in that section one Sunday, a man lay prostrate in the middle of the road in a hot noonday sun. "He's drunk," said the sheriff. "I guess I'd better stick him in the calaboose."

"He ain't drunk at all," disputed a fellow townsman. "I jest seen his fingers move."

»»*««

A MAGICIAN had a marked fondness for rabbit stew which the rabbit stew never reciprocated. In the middle of one dinner, the magician had a hurried exit. The waiter watched him rush out and chuckled, "By golly, that's the first time I ever saw a rabbit make a magician disappear."

»»✳«

A LOVELY little old lady contributed a pair of pajamas to the Red Cross. "I made them myself," she said proudly. They were perfect in every detail, except that there was no opening in the front of the pants. When the inspector explained the error, the old lady's face fell. Suddenly she brightened. "Couldn't you give them to a bachelor?" she suggested.

»»✳«

THE PASTOR frowned thoughtfully and said, "Son, haven't I seen you some place before?" "You have indeed," said his visitor. "I've come to ask you if you think it right to profit by the mistakes of others." "Certainly not," said the pastor vehemently. "Good," said the visitor. "In that case, how about giving me back the ten spot I paid you six months ago for performing my marriage ceremony?"

»»✳«

MILTON BERLE told his radio audience that his sponsor had gifted him at Christmas with a one-hundred-and-fourteen-piece after-dinner set—a box of toothpicks.

Berle added that he had hung up his stocking dutifully on Christmas Eve. The only thing he found in it the next morning was a summons from the health department.

»»✳«

A TRAVELING SALESMAN came to a hotel and asked for a room for the night. He pleaded desperately upon being told, "Sorry"—after all, there wasn't another hotel for miles. Finally, he offered to share a room. At that the clerk said, "Colonel Bumple, in Room 1203, is not using one of the beds

(93)

in his room. I'll ask him." The Colonel agreed readily and the salesman left instructions to be awakened at 6:30 A.M. as he had to make a 7 o'clock train. He slept well.

The next morning, going down in the elevator, he was greeted by the attendant with a "Good morning, Colonel Bumple." Passing the room clerk he looked back at hearing, "Good morning, Colonel Bumple." The doorman—this time he was positive—did the same. He passed off these greetings with a shrug, murmuring to himself, "At 6:30 A.M. no one is in his right senses." On boarding the train he went to the washroom, looked in the mirror, and decided he needed a shave. A second look and he let out a scream. The train was already on its way. The passengers were perplexed as he went dashing madly down the aisle yelling frantically, "My God! They woke up the wrong man!"

»»*««

THE ARITHMETIC TEACHER said, "Now, boys, I want you to figure what interest of one percent on a million dollars for two years would come to." The whole class set to work diligently with the exception of little Mawruss in the front row. "What's the matter, Mawruss?" said the teacher. "One percent doesn't interest me," said Mawruss.

»»*««

MARX FANS like to remember when Groucho was playing Dr. Something-or-other and took Mrs. Rittenhouse's pulse. "My dear woman," he said with infinite pity, "you have mice!"

An intern interrupted to report, "There's a man outside with a black moustache."

"Tell him I've got one," snapped Groucho.

»»*««

TWO TACITURN Maine farmers had known each other all their

lives, but their conversations were usually restricted to "Mornin' " or "Nice day." One afternoon, however, the first farmer grew a bit more loquacious. "Hi, Luke," he asked, "what did you give your horse when he had the colic?"

"Turpentine," said Luke.

'Thanks," said his friend.

Two weeks later they met again. "Didn't you tell me, Luke, that you gave your horse turpentine when he had the colic?"

"Yup," said Luke.

"Well, I gave mine turpentine and he died."

"So did mine," said Luke.

»»✲««

"I SEE your lass has got herself a mon," said Mrs. MacGregor to Mrs. MacTavish.

"Aye, that she has."

"Is it working well?"

"Well enough. Verra well, in fact. Of course, she canna bide her mon, but then, isn't there always something?"

»»✲««

LEVENTHAL SIGNED up as motorman on the Spring Street crosstown. His run was short and poorly patronized. The first time he took the car out he was back in nineteen minutes with a dollar ten in fares. The second time he completed his run in eighteen and a half minutes and rang up ninety cents. Then he disappeared for a solid three hours.

Just as the superintendent was about to report to the police, Leventhal turned up, all smiles, with receipts of eighteen sixty-five. "Business was so bad on Spring Street," he explained, "that I took the car up Broadway."

(95)

AN EAST SIDE synagogue reaped its greatest harvest on the Jewish New Year holidays when every seat was sold months in advance, and enough money was raised to take care of several special charities for the balance of the year. One morning, in the middle of the services, a man came dashing up to the door of the synagogue and rushed past the gatekeeper. "Hey," cried that dignitary, "you can't get in here without a ticket."

"You don't understand," said the intruder. "My partner, Rosenthal, is in there, and I've got to tell him that our store is burning down."

The gatekeeper considered for a moment, and then allowed, "All right, I will let you go in long enough to tell Rosenthal. But don't let me catch you praying."

»»*««

YOUNG BRISCOW got a job in a bank. The cashier tossed him a package of one-dollar bills and said, "Check them to make sure there are one hundred." Briscow started counting. Finally he got up to "56," "57," "58." Then he threw the package in the drawer. "If it is right this far," he remarked to the man next to him, "it is probably right all the way."

»»*««

"I AM OFF to the races," said Mr. Dale to his wife, "and I only hope I break even. I sure need the dough."

»»*««

A FATHER shook his head sadly as his son left the room. For the fourth successive month his report card had shown nothing but D's. "I am finally convinced," he told his wife, "that our son must have a sixth sense. There's certainly no sign of the other five."

(96)

WHEN CALVIN COOLIDGE was a boy, a chum tried to borrow a five-spot from him—and was turned down. When Coolidge was President the same party visited the White House, and renewed his request for a five-dollar loan. Again Coolidge refused. The chum drawled, in reluctant admiration, "I got to hand it to you, Cal; success ain't changed you a bit!"

»»✳«««

CLANCY RUSHED into Sullivan's Tavern and cried, "Timmy, me bucko, give me three whiskeys before the trouble starts." Sullivan gave him the drinks and said, "Now then, Mike, what's the trouble and when does it start?" "Right now," Clancy assured him. "I ain't got a penny in me pocket!"

»»✳«««

IF YOU WANT to make an unexpected guest comfortable at the dinner table, this is a good story not to tell him.

A man who lived three miles from the main road outside of Newburgh left his house one afternoon, walked until he caught a bus, and rode on it to the Newburgh ferry station. He took a ferry to Beacon, another bus to the railroad station, and a local train to Grand Central. There he transferred to a subway train for the end of the line at New Lots Avenue, Brooklyn, where another bus carried him nine or ten miles farther. A brisk twenty-minute walk brought him to a solitary apartment house, where he climbed six flights of stairs and rang the bell of his friends, the Heimerdingers, just as they were sitting down to dinner.

"For goodness sake," said Mrs. Heimerdinger, "what brings you here at this hour of the night?"

"Oh," he replied vaguely, "I just happened to be in the neighborhood."

(97)

TWO DRUNKS in a mid-town bar were discussing life: "I had the darndest dream last night," said one. "I dreamed that suddenly about one thousand funny little men were dancing on top of my body. They had pink caps and green suits and funny red boots that curled up in the front."

"Yes," agreed the other, "and there was a tinkly little bell at the toe of each of the boots."

"How do you know?" said the first one in surprise.

"There are a couple of them still sitting on your shoulder," said the other.

»»✳««

THERE ONCE was a little tailor named Kuhn who had a big sign in his window which read, "Moshe Kuhn, formerly of Kuhn, Loeb & Co." At that time the late Otto Kahn was the head of the famous banking house of Kuhn, Loeb & Co., and his friends twitted him so much about the tailor's sign that Kahn finally visited the tailor shop himself.

"You know very well that you are making this story up," he chided. "I will give you $100 if you will take that sign out of your window."

The tailor agreed with alacrity. The next day Mr. Kahn came by to see if he had lived up to his bargain. Sure enough, the offending sign had disappeared. In its place was one twice as large which read, "Moshe Kuhn: absolutely no connection with Kuhn, Loeb & Co."

»»✳««

A VILLAGE PASTOR stopped a little nine-year-old girl on the street one day and said, "Well, well, Mary, I hear God has just sent you two little twin brothers."

(98)

"Yes, he did," said little Mary. "And he knows where the money's coming from too. Daddy said so."

»»*««

EVERYBODY COMMENTED on how bravely Mr. Casey took his wife's sudden death. Dry-eyed and composed, he superintended personally all the details of her funeral. As the pallbearers were carrying the coffin through the cemetery gate, one of them accidentally banged his corner of the coffin into a post. It turned out that Mrs. Casey was not quite dead. The sudden jar brought her back to consciousness and there came from the inside of the coffin a muffled scream. Of course they rushed her back to the hospital where she lingered for ten anxious days. Then she really died. Again the funeral procession wended its way to the cemetery. As they were carrying the coffin through the gate, Mr. Casey cried in a loud voice, "For the love of Mike, look out for that post!"

»»*««

THE DEER-HUNTING set likes to recall Ed Wynn's routine when, just before going out to stalk a moose or two, he caught sight of himself in a full-length mirror, gasped in horror, and exclaimed, "Thank God I'm out of season."

»»*««

WHEN THE Ziegfeld Follies were at the height of their fame, Florenz Ziegfeld met a Middle-Western merchant whom he had known in his childhood and, as a special treat, took him to a rehearsal of the new production for that year. One beautiful girl after another came out on the stage in a scant rehearsal costume. The merchant stared intently but all he said was an occasional "Phui." Ziegfeld, very annoyed, finally said, "I simply can't understand you. Here I show you some of the most beautiful girls in America with practically no clothes on, and all you do is sit here and say 'phui.' "

"I wasn't thinking of the girls," said the merchant sadly. "I was thinking of my wife."

»»*««

AN ENGLISHMAN arrived in America for his first visit and a New York publisher, bursting with local pride, took him uptown in an open car. "There is the Municipal Building," he pointed out. "It's sort of our City Hall. American workmen put up the whole building in 132 days."

"That's not very remarkable," said the Londoner. "Our City Hall was built in ninety-four days."

A little later the New Yorker pointed out the Williamsburg Bridge. They built that in four months flat," he boasted.

"Our new Waterloo Bridge," answered the Englishman, "was put up in two months and a half."

The New Yorker pointed out several other architectural triumphs, but the Englishman topped him every time. By this time the New Yorker was considerably nettled. Suddenly the Englishman gasped in surprise as their car passed by the Empire State Building. "What's the name of that building?" he inquired.

The American shrugged his shoulders. "I couldn't tell you," he said. "It wasn't there when I came downtown this morning."

»»*««

TWO SOUR-PUSS farmers like to grumble to each other. "Never did see hay grow so short as mine this summer," sighed one. "You think yours is short," answered the other. "I had to lather mine to mow it!"

»»✲««

IN THE middle of the depression, the owner of a big shoe factory was summoned by the vice president of the local bank. "About that loan of two hundred thousand," began the banker.

The manufacturer interrupted. "Mr. Austrian, what do you know about the shoe business?" he asked.

"Frankly, nothing," said the banker, distinctly nettled.

"Better learn it fast, brother," said the manufacturer. "You're in it."

»»✲««

A PROMINENT CITIZEN was confined in a Carolina hospital for several weeks and was served so faithfully by a Negro orderly named Ben that he gave him an unusually big tip the day he got out. Ben was overwhelmed, and felt he must pay a compliment in return. He gulped hard and produced a "We is goin' to miss you terribly around here, Mr. Walker. You sho does take a good enema."

»»✲««

"I'M AFRAID we're going to have to fire that new salesman," the manager told his boss at a morning conference. "I made a few suggestions to him yesterday and he flew into a rage. I told him I'd report his language to you and he said, 'You can tell that old poop to go to Hackensack and back.' "

"Hmm," said the boss. "How much did he sell on his last trip?"

"Oh, he did very well," conceded the sales manager. "We had never gotten more than $20,000 out of that territory, but on his first swing around he rang up a total of $50,000."

"In that case," said the boss, "I suggest that we ascertain the price of a round-trip ticket to Hackensack."

»»*««

WARNER BROS. recently hit upon a bright new idea for arousing advance interest in a new Humphrey Bogart thriller. They ordered posters in subway stations that bore only the words: "This space reserved for Humphrey Bogart." Two days after the poster went out, they got a letter from an indignant fan. "What a cheap, dirty trick," he wrote. "How can anybody draw a moustache on a sign like that?"

»»*««

A MOTORCYCLE COP strode back to the sedan he had flagged. "Hey," he bellowed to the cringing figure at the wheel. "I am arresting you on four counts. In the first place, you drove through a red light back on Central Avenue. In the second place, you are going the wrong way on a one-way street. In the third place, you've been tearing through the center of town at 50 miles an hour. And in the fourth place, you didn't pay any attention to my siren for fully ten blocks."

The driver's wife leaned across her silent husband and gave the cop her sweetest smile. "You really mustn't mind him, Officer," she cooed. "He's dead drunk."

»»*««

"THIS IS the Duke of Whoopingham's estate," said the guide from Cook's, and added sotto voce, "One of our great landed proprietors, ya' know."

A young lady from Newark expressed sudden interest. "Who landed him?" she inquired.

ARTHUR KOBER, author of *My Dear Bella,* tells about the day when Mrs. Gross met Mrs. Shlepkin on the Grand Concourse. Mrs. Shlepkin looked so downcast that Mrs. Gross cried, "For God's sake, Sadie, what's the trouble?"

"Mine poor husband," sighed Mrs. Shlepkin. "The doctor just told him he has cancer."

"Is that all," said Mrs. Gross, slapping Mrs. Shlepkin heartily on the back. "So what are you worrying about? Cancer, shmancer, as long as he's got his health."

»»✳««

McWHORTLE EXPRESSED himself as highly sympathetic to the viewpoint and aims of the Gleneagles Anti-Tipping Society, but his enthusiasm waned perceptibly when he heard the annual dues were two shillings a year. "Two shillings," he grumbled. "Mon, I can save money at that figure by going on tippin' right through the year."

»»✳««

A DETERMINED-LOOKING gent strode into a Western Union office, dashed off a telegram, and stamped his foot impatiently while the clerk counted the words. "You've only got nine words in this telegram," said the clerk. "You are entitled to one more without extra charge."

Together the man and the clerk reread the telegram which went as follows: "Galumph, galumph, galumph, galumph, galumph, galumph, galumph, galumph, galumph."

"I can't think of another word to add," said the man.

"Why not another galumph?" suggested the clerk.

"Another galumph?" said the man angrily. "That would be silly."

A horse walked up to a bar and asked for a martini with catsup. "Okay, bud," said the bartender, and mixed it pronto. After tossing off the drink with considerable and obvious relish, the horse leaned over the bar and said, "I suppose you think it is strange that a horse should come in here and ask for a martini with catsup in it." "Hell, no," said the bartender. "I like them that way myself."

There is another story that runs along similar lines about a sailor who cabled his best girl from Honolulu. *His* message read, "I love you, I love you, I love you." When he learned that he could have a tenth word without extra charge, he gave the matter a great deal of thought, and then added "Regards."

RASTUS HAD been operating an elevator at Macey's for thirty years, but this was absolutely the first time that anybody had ever tried to enter it leading a horse by a short piece of rope. "You can't bring that horse in here," said Rastus indignantly.

"Have a heart," begged the man. "I've simply got to take him up in the elevator."

"You do," said Rastus. "*Why?*"

"Because," said the man, "he always gets sick on the escalator."

»»*««

MISS FRASER was surprised to get a telephone call at her home from the teller at her bank. "I'm sorry to tell you," said the teller, "that as of February 1st your account is overdrawn by more than $200."

"How much did I have in your bank on January 1st?" countered Miss Fraser.

"$600," said the teller.

"And how much was there on December 1st?"

"Over $1000," the teller replied.

"Then why do you call me in February?" said Miss Fraser triumphantly. "Did *I* call *you* in January or December?"

»»*««

THREE GIRLS gathered in a small restaurant for lunch. "I think I'll have a chicken sandwich," said the first one, "with white meat."

"White meat isn't good for a young girl," said the waiter. "Take roast beef."

"Okay," said the girl. "Roast beef I like."

"Better make it whole wheat," said the waiter. "It's got more vitamins."

The second girl picked corned beef hash. "Don't take that," said the waiter. "It's made up of all the things that other people leave on their plates. The London broil is what you should take."

"All right," said the second girl. "Make it London broil, and a cup of coffee."

"Coffee," exclaimed the waiter. "You won't sleep a wink tonight. You take a nice glass of fresh buttermilk."

"Very well," said the girl. "London broil and buttermilk it is."

The third girl looked timidly at the waiter. "What do you think I ought to order?" she said.

"How do I know?" said the waiter indignantly. "Who's got time around here to make suggestions?"

»»*««

A JUDGE eyed his prisoner disapprovingly and said, "Why did you beat your wife?"

"It was a sudden impulse," explained the prisoner.

"Very well," said the judge. "On a sudden impulse I am going to put you in the cooler for thirty days."

"Okay," said the prisoner sadly. "But you are certainly putting a crimp in our honeymoon."

»»*««

A WOULD-BE Broadway producer, operating on a shoestring, was interviewing applicants for the heroine's part. One girl delighted him. "You're just what the doctor ordered," he told her. "Right face, right coloring, right voice, everything called for in the part. By the way, what's your salary?"

"$600 a week," said the girl.

"Sorry," snapped the producer. "You're too tall."

(106)

ONE OF THE most famous pieces of dramatic criticism ever penned appeared in an English newspaper the day after a local stock company had essayed a presentation of *Hamlet*. "For some time," read the notice, "there has been a controversy as to whether Shakespeare or Sir Francis Bacon actually wrote the plays attributed to the former. Now at last this column is in a position to settle the question once and for all. Let the tombs of both men be opened. The one who turned over last night is the true author of *Hamlet*."

»»*««

NEAL O'HARA tells about a dry-goods proprietor whose store burned to the ground the very day that he signed a new fire-insurance policy. The company suspected fraud, but had no proof. The only thing the manager could do was to write the policy holder the following note: "Sir: You took out an insurance policy from us at 10 A.M. and your fire did not break out until 3:30 P.M. Will you kindly explain the delay?"

»»*««

"WAITER," said a testy patron. "I must say I don't like all the flies in this dining room."

"Tell me which ones you don't like," said the conciliatory waiter, "and I'll chase them out for you."

»»*««

WHEN KERRIGAN and Fitzgerald made their first trip to Paris, they were very much impressed with the sights, but stuck firmly to their resolve to have no truck whatever with French girls. One evening, however, Kerrigan could find no Irish girl to escort on the rounds of the Montmartre night clubs and grudgingly consented to convoy a very beautiful and chic Parisienne. The next morning Fitzgerald could hardly

(107)

wait to ask Kerrigan what kind of a time he had had. "Fitz-gerald, me boy," said Kerrigan with a satisfied sigh. "You kin quote me to the iffect that sex is in its infancy."

»»✳««

THE SERVANT PROBLEM being what it is, a wealthy young housewife was delighted to hear that a strong and willing girl had just arrived from Lapland and was looking for a job. The girl readily consented to an interview, but it developed that she could neither cook, clean, take care of the children, nor do the laundry. The baffled housewife said, "But my dear, what *can* you do?"

The young Lap proudly answered, "I can milk reindeer."

»»✳««

A MUSICAL COMEDY producer explained the chief differences between Al Jolson, Eddie Cantor, and George Jessel. "Jolson," said the producer, "has six million dollars and is worried that he is going to lose it. Cantor hasn't got six million dollars and is worried that he isn't going to get it. Jessel is worried that Cantor is going to get it."

»»✳««

CHARLES LEE, the demon Philadelphia book reviewer, knows an old Irish lady who was making a trip between Northern Ireland and Eire, and was stopped at the boundary line by a stern customs official. She declared that the only thing she had with her was a bottle of water. "What kind of water?" asked the official.

"A bottle of holy water from Lourdes," said the lady evenly.

The inspector had had experience with bottles before. He

snatched this one out of the old lady's hand, pulled open the cork and got a whiff of the contents. "It's whiskey," he declared triumphantly.

The old lady rolled her eyes toward heaven and murmured in reverent tones, "Glory be to God! It's a miracle!"

»»*««

AN AMERICAN REPORTER found an old Frenchman in a chateau who was quite hale and hearty though he admitted to 105 years. "Good eating and good drinking is what has preserved me," he told the reporter. "Wine is the only beverage for a sensible human being. Why am I in such perfect health? Because not a drop of water has ever passed my lips."

"I can't quite believe that," laughed the reporter. "Don't you ever brush your teeth in the morning?"

"For that," replied the old gentleman gravely, "I use a light sauterne."

»»*««

A GREAT SCIENTIST had finished his lecture to a Bronxville ladies' club and the members were buzzing around him as he descended from the podium.

"Professor," gushed one lady, "we've been hearing a lot about these new lie detectors. Have you ever seen one in action?"

"Seen one!" snapped the Professor. "I married one!"

»»*««

A COUNTY BUMPKIN watched his cousin breathing his last, and suddenly darted from the room. He came back carrying a heavy dining-room chair.

"What's that for?" asked the doctor.

"That," said the bumpkin, "is for Rigor Mortis to set in."

(109)

HOWARD DIETZ, publicity director of MGM, was complaining to a meeting of motion-picture exhibitors about the growing tendency to give the public too much for its money. "I will tell you how far things have gone," he said. "I just heard about a man in Oklahoma who went to a theatre where, for fifteen cents, he got two feature pictures, a Micky Mouse, a newsreel, and two sets of dishes, and then demanded his money back because he didn't strike oil under his seat."

»»✳««

INCIDENTALLY, there was an amusing aftermath to this story which will indicate how difficult it is to trace funny stories back to their original source. George Jessel, the famous comedian, heard Dietz tell the story and used it himself on a radio program a few nights later with gratifying results. Several weeks later, Dietz used the story again in a magazine article. When Jessel read it, he wired Dietz: "How come you're crabbing my material?"

»»✳««

TWO CHORUS GIRLS were calmly chopping an absent mutual "friend" into tiny bits.

"What annoys me about Mayme," said the first, "is she ain't got no modesty. She's a shrieking violet."

"Yeah," agreed the second. "She minds her own business— at the top of her voice."

»»✳««

TWO OLD MAID monkeys were chattering in a forest primeval. "Just look at that deer making a fool of herself for two bucks," said one. The other sighed, "I could use a little doe myself."

A PROMINENT Turkish-paste man promoted an audience with the Sultan. "I don't think I recall your name," said the Sultan pleasantly, "but your fez is familiar."

»»*««

"I CAN'T imagine," said an indignant lady to an alienist, "why my family has insisted upon dragging me to see you. What's wrong with loving pancakes?"

"Nothing at all," agreed the alienist, rather surprised. "I like pancakes myself."

"Goody, goody," said the lady. "You must come up to my house and let me show you my collection. I've got trunks and trunks full of them."

»»*««

THE IMPRESSIVE-LOOKING party in the striped trousers and the frock coat stepped solemnly to the bar. "I say, old man," he mouthed from under a walrus mustache. "Nip me up a spot of whiskey with a dash of Pims Number One."

"I don't get you," said the bartender.

The party repeated his order impatiently. "I'm afraid I still don't know what you're talking about," said the barkeep. "I guess you're English, aren't you?"

"My dear fellow," said the customer, with some dignity, "if I were any more English I couldn't even talk."

»»*««

ON THE overnight boat from Ireland to England, a passenger accosted a uniformed character at the rail: "I say, are you the mate?"

"That Oi'm not," answered the character. "Oi'm the man that cooks the mate."

"I SIMPLY gotta divorce this woman," the disconsolate man explained to the court. "She insisted upon keeping a pet goat in our bedroom. The smell got so terrible I just couldn't stand it any longer."

The judge shook his head. "That sounds bad," he admitted, "but couldn't you open a window?"

"What?" cried the husband. "And let all my pigeons get out?"

»»*««

A PRETTY young newlywed awoke early one morning and shook her husband until he awoke with a start. "What's the matter, darling?" he inquired hazily.

"Henry Jones," she said firmly, "if I dream once more that you've kissed another woman, I will never talk to you again as long as I live."

»»*««

WEBER WAS trying to sell his old pal Fields some accident insurance. "Today you flit happy as a butterscotch from flower to flower," he pointed out. "Tomorrow you may be lying prostrate in der gutter."

Fields looked skeptical. "Take Meyer," persisted Weber. "Der day after he took out a $10,000 policy, he had both legs and both arms cut off in an auto accident."

"I know," said Fields. "But he vas vun of der lucky vuns."

»»*««

A WESTERN CONGRESSMAN was recently defeated in his fight for re-election. He inserted the following ad in his local newspaper: "I wish to thank all those who voted for me, and my wife wishes to thank all those who didn't."

(112)

A MOTORIST was pushing his stalled sedan up a hill, perspiring freely, and cussing like a trooper. A person overheard him and remarked, "Swearing, sir, will avail you nothing. Had you tried prayer, your motor might have responded."

"Oh, yeah?" said the motorist. "Let's see you do it, wise guy."

The parson felt he could not sidestep the challenge. Kneeling on the curb, he prayed, "O Lord, make the car of this poor sinner run under its own power." Then he climbed into the front seat and gingerly pressed his foot on the starter. The motor coughed once or twice, and then began to purr as smoothly as the catalogue said it would. The two men listened entranced. "Well, I'll be damned," said the parson.

»»*««

ONE OF THE houses that was completely demolished by a recent catastrophic explosion near Cleveland belonged to a widow who lived all alone. She herself was uninjured. A doctor who rushed to the scene told her that one of the few things that had not been destroyed in her house was a bottle of brandy, and he suggested that she take a nip of it to steady her nerves. "Nothing doing," said the widow. "I'm saving that for an emergency."

»»*««

THE ATLANTA PENITENTIARY will be playing host for the next twenty years to the most expert and also the most egotistical counterfeiter of his day. He made $5 bills more perfectly than the mint itself. Unfortunately, he couldn't resist one slight innovation. Instead of Lincoln's picture, he insisted upon using his own.

A KENTUCKY HILLBILLY watched his wife cooking victuals. "Better move a mite, maw," he suggested. "You be standing on a live coal."

"Do tell," said maw. "Which foot?"

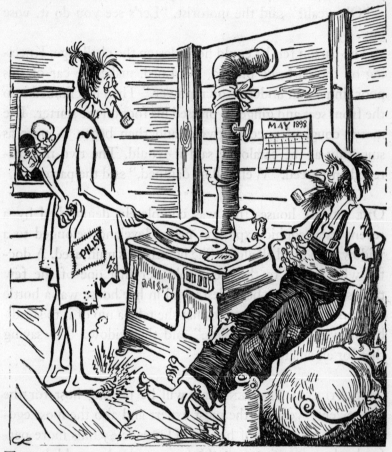

THE CARNIVAL BARKER pounded his chest vigorously and said, "Look what this wonderful snake oil has done for me, ladies and gentlemen. Note my marvelous constitution.

Would you possibly guess that I am over 200 years old, and was one of the original Minute Men at Concord?"

A farmer seemed somewhat skeptical and buttonholed the barker's assistant. "Is he really that old?" he asked.

"You can't prove it by me," said the assistant. "I've only been working for him 120 years."

»»✻««

VOICE ON THE PHONE: Is this the Salvation Army?

Answer: Yes, it is.

Voice: Is it true that you save young girls?

Answer: Yes, it is.

Voice: Well, please save me one for Saturday night."

»»✻««

AN INEBRIATED GENT wandered by accident into the cemetery where a funeral service was in progress. He stood silently by until the officiating minister intoned, "Ashes to ashes, dust to dust." The inebriated gent nodded solemnly and, in a loud voice, inquired, "Could anything be fairer than that?"

»»✻««

"YES, INDEEDY," boasted Sister Jones, "Ah has fo' fine sons! Eeenie, Meenie, Minie, and Frankie."

"Why Frankie?" asked the visitor. "After Sinatra?"

"Partly," said Sister Jones. "But princip'ly 'cause we don' want no Mo!"

»»✻««

A LONDON DOWAGER, very hard of hearing, visited her niece in Edinburgh, and went with her to church on Sunday. The deacon at the door eyed her ear-trumpet with deep suspicion. He tapped her on the shoulder and reminded her, "One toot and ye're oot!"

AT EVERY STOP of the Los Angeles-New York plane, a red gasoline truck dashed onto the field to replenish the fuel supply. At the Washington airport a passenger said to the young lady seated beside him, "This plane sure does make time, doesn't it?" "It certainly does," she agreed, "but that red truck seems to keep right up with us!"

»»*««

GORDON WAS a happily married man, but when a beautiful blonde in the hotel lobby gave him the business, he went the way of all flesh, and forgot all about the convention he was supposed to be attending. A few weeks later a sinister-looking party with a suspicious bulge in his right-hand pocket muscled into Gordon's inner sanctum. "Bud, about dis week-end wid me goil friend in Atlantic City," he began, out of the corner of his mouth. "It just so happens we gotta coupla pitchers of the two of yez down dere." He spread six compromising photographs on Gordon's desk and stood back to observe the effect. Gordon responded immediately. "Beautiful! Simply beautiful!" he beamed. "I'll take three each of the first five and half a dozen of the last one!"

»»*««

THE DENTIST stood back and shook his head at the young thing in the chair. "My dear," he said. "I don't like to tell you this, but you've got acute pyorrhea." "Never mind that now, Doctor," snapped the young thing. "Just get on with your dentistry."

»»*««

FRED ALLEN knows a man who is such a heel that his stocking hangs *him* up for Christmas.

(116)

THE BEGGAR flaunting the "Please Help the Blind" sign looked so forlorn that the lady fished in her bag and handed him a two-dollar bill.

"Sorry, lady," he said. "Two-dollar bills is bad luck. Ain't you got two singles?"

"How did you know it was a two-dollar bill if you're blind?"

"I ain't blind, lady. My partner's blind. It's his day off, so he's gone to the movies and I'm pinchhittin' for him. Me, I'm a deaf mute."

»»✳««

A LAWYER, a doctor, an architect, and an ardent American communist were lunching at Luchow's, and fell to arguing over which profession had been established first in the world. "A lawyer, of course," said the first. "Man could never have survived without a few simple laws to govern him."

"Nuts," said the doctor. "Without a gynecologist, how could Cain and Abel have been born?"

The architect sneered. "Long before that, my friends, before Adam and Eve, some architect must have been on the job to bring order out of the chaos."

"Ah, ha!" beamed the communist. "*And who created the chaos?*"

»»✳««

A SENTIMENTAL LADY on a tour of the Oregon State campus stopped before a gigantic tree. "O wonderful elm," she said, "if you could only speak, what would you say to me?"

The senior forester accompanying her suggested, "It would probably say, 'Pardon me, but I'm an oak.'"

A PATIENT was ushered into a famous psychiatrist's office. "I've got a strange hallucination," he said. "I keep imagining that horrible little black bugs are crawling over me. Look here are a couple of hundred of them on my arm right now."

The psychiatrist blanched and pushed the patient away. "For God's sake, keep your distance," he cried. "You'll get them all over me."

»»*««

PAT HURLEY swears that in the part of Oklahoma he hails from, there's so little water that you can tell when a school of fish is swimming upriver by the cloud of dust it raises.

»»*««

THE PRINCIPAL of a school in the Kentucky moonshine country asked a gangly scholar, "How much is seven and seven?" "Ten," hazarded the scholar. "Well, I'll mark you passing," said the principal, "seein' as how you only missed it by one."

»»*««

TWO VETERANS of World War One met in Baltimore. "Remember that saltpeter they used to put into our food in Camp Lee in 1918?" asked one. "I sure do," said the other. "It's starting to take effect now," mourned the first.

»»*««

ONE OF THE great story-tellers of our day is Harry Hershfield. His biggest laugh at a recent dinner was scored with the story of Mandelbaum in a drugstore. "I need medicine but I lost it the proscreepshun," he told the druggist. "Can you remember the name of the medicine?" "It sounds like some beeg city." "New York? London? Liverpool?" "Dot's it! Carter's Little Liverpools."

(118)

ANOTHER HERSHFIELD classic: A henpecked husband was only allowed to play in nickel-limit poker games. One night he broke bounds and lost twenty-five dollars. "My wife will kill me," he moaned to a friend. "If you don't lend me the money, I'll never be able to go home." His friend gave him the twenty-five. A few moments later he was back. "I had a happy thought," he said. "Couldn't you lend me ten dollars more? I'd like to prove to her I was the big winner."

»»✷««

ROBERT BROWNING'S most obscure and difficult poem is "Sordello." One of its passages baffled even the London Poetry Society. They asked him to explain it. Browning read it over twice, shrugged his shoulders, and said, "When I wrote that, God and I knew what it meant, but now God alone knows."

»»✷««

AN ENGLISHMAN was out fishing with a Maine guide one morning and had an exceptionally good run of luck. "What a jolly outing!" he exclaimed. "Do you think we'll be able to find this exact spot again tomorrow?"

"I'll tell you what we'll do," said the guide grumpily. "We'll put a cross on the bow of the boat so we'll know just where to come."

The Englishman pondered over this for a few moments and said, "I'm afraid that won't do, old chap. Supposing we can't find this boat in the morning?"

»»✷««

FEMININE VOICE over telephone: Hello, are you Harry?

Masculine voice: Not especially, lady, but I am far from bald.

(119)

A SMART MERCHANT on 14th Street put a display of new evening dresses in his window, along with the following sign: "These dresses are built like a fence. They protect the property but do not obstruct the view."

»»*««

A MAN who had never before spent a night on a train took the Owl from New York to Boston. Just before the train reached South Station, the porter brushed his coat. "What's the average tip on this train?" asked the traveler.

"Two dollars," said the porter promptly.

The traveler gave him $2 and said, "You must make quite a lot of money on this job."

"Not as much as you might think," said the porter. "You is de first average I'se had in six months."

»»*««

"MY GRANDFATHER," boasted a nouveau-riche from Commonwealth Avenue, "fought in the Zulu War."

"You don't say," drawled a Beacon Hillite. "On which side?"

»»*««

"SPEAKING OF bathing in famous springs," said the tramp to the tourist, "I bathed in the spring of '86."

»»*««

MOSE DROPPED a quarter on the street, but after a half hour's search he was unable to find it. His companion inquired, "Say, son, wasn't you able to find that two bits?"

"No, I wasn't," the victim replied, "but I might have if you hadn't helped me so much."

A TOASTMASTER who entertained a healthy loathing for the guest of honor introduced him as "Good old Peabody. You have only to put a dinner in his mouth, and out comes a speech."

Peabody jumped to his feet and began, "First let us pause long enough to consider our genial toastmaster. As you may have observed, you have only to put a speech in his mouth, and out comes your dinner!"

»»*««

A BEAUTIFUL young bride of a month greeted her husband one evening with a particularly happy smile. "Your dinner is going to be different tonight, darling," she said. "A neighbor just told me that you have to add water to those dehydrated foods."

»»*««

A CAPTAIN and a lieutenant were dining at the Stork Club when a corporal entered escorting a ravishingly beautiful damsel. The captain, a Lycanthropist of sorts (Lycanthropist: one who suffers from the delusion that he is a wolf), sent a note to the corporal: "The Lieutenant, who is a Princeton man, and I, who hail from Williams, bet a fin we could guess the college you come from. May we stop at your table and see who was right?"

Back came the reply: "Please don't bother, gentlemen. I am from the Audubon Institute of Ornithology, and I intend to classify this pigeon myself."

»»*««

"Now WILLIE," coaxed Mama, "be a good boy and say 'Ah-h-h,' so the nasty doctor can get his finger out of your mouth."

A GIRL and her aunt worked in an aircraft factory. A thug grabbed their salary envelopes one day. The girl found a cop and gasped, "I've been robbed of my pay and my aunt's pay." "Cut out the pig-Latin," suggested the cop, "and tell me what really happened."

»»✳««

A TYPOGRAPHER's Christmas card to his daughter:
   Girls who eat their spinach have legs like this: !!
   Girls who ride horseback have legs like this: ()
   Girls who get drunk have legs like this:) (
   And girls who use good judgment have legs like this: X
   (The daughter sent it to Walter Winchell and achieved immortality.)

»»✳««

A FRIEND asked George Jessel, "How's your Ma?" "Terrible," said George. "She's got chronic frontal sinusitis." "Good Lord, where did she get that?" "From *Reader's Digest*. She read about it last month."

»»✳««

A WORRIED LADY drove a rather battered Buick into a garage. "Do you think you can fix these front fenders so my husband won't know I banged them up?" she inquired anxiously.

   The experienced garage man said, "We can't do that, lady, but we can fix them so that you can ask him tomorrow what in heck he did to them."

»»✳««

A FAMOUS NOVELIST's agent wore a deep frown all evening. Finally the novelist asked what was troubling him. "It's a dream I had last night," the agent said. "I dreamed that you wrote a novel that was chosen by the Book-of-the-Month Club, sold over a million copies and was bought by MGM for $500,000."

"What's so terrible about that?" said the novelist.

The agent shook his head sadly. "I woke up," he said, "just before I collected my 10% commission."

»»✳««

"MY FATHER and mother were first cousins," the new pupil explained to his teacher. "I guess that's why I look so much alike."

»»✳««

"I LEFT a bottle of bonded scotch on the 8:15 this morning," an unhappy commuter told the attendant at the lost-and-found window. "Are you sure nobody turned it in?" "Nope," said the attendant. "Your bottle isn't here. But if you wait a minute, I think we've got the guy who found it."

»»✳««

TWO BEARDED Polish merchants met at the Warsaw station. "Where are you bound for?" asked the first. "Minsk," was the answer.

"Ah ha!" snorted the other. "You don't fool me for a second. You tell me Minsk so I should think you are going to Pinsk. All the time I know perfectly well you're going to Minsk!"

»»✳««

"MY WOODEN LEG is giving me a lot of pain," sighed the patient. "How can a wooden leg give you pain?" the doctor asked. The patient explained, "My wife hit me over the head with it."

GREENBAUM SOUGHT out the proprietor of the Idle Hour delicatessen and said, "The food by the Idle Hour is wary good, mine friend, but why are you so stingy with de brad? Every night you give me only two slices brad."

The next night the proprietor saw that he had three slices of bread on his platter, but Greenbaum grumbled again as he paid his check, "Only three slices brad." Four slices the next night and five slices the night after still failed to satisfy

him. Finally, when he came marching into the delicatessen on Saturday night, the proprietor whispered to the waiter. "Here comes that kicker Greenbaum again. Take a long French loaf of bread, cut it in two, and shut him up once and for all."

The bread that the waiter dug up for Greenbaum was fully five feet long. As he paid his check, the proprietor smiled at him and said, "Well, Mr. Greenbaum, I hope everything was all right tonight."

"All right!" barked Mr. Greenbaum. "I see you're back to two slices brad."

»»✳««

"SPIKE" WARREN was not only the toughest character in town, but he had a particular grievance against the *Daily Blast*. When the *Blast* editor sent his greenest cub reporter out to interview "Spike," therefore, the staff sat back to await developments. They were soon forthcoming.

The cub phoned the editor and said, "When Warren found out who I was, he punched me in the nose and kicked me downstairs." "Damn it all, go up again," roared the editor.

Fifteen minutes later, the cub was back on the phone, though his voice was feebler. "This time," he reported, "Warren knocked out three of my teeth, blackened both eyes, and kicked me downstairs again." "He did, did he?" shouted the editor. "Well, you just keep going back till he gives you an interview. I'll teach that yellow s. of a b. that he can't intimidate *me!*"

»»✳««

Ross MADE a killing in Santa Fe common, and his wife decided it was time to polish his rough edges. His worst fault, she told him, was that he bellowed every remark at the top of his lungs. When he whispered, pictures trembled on walls a block away. Ross promised to modulate his voice.

One day a fire broke out in his house, and his wife, coming home from a matinee, saw him outlined in an eighth-story window, hollering "Help! Save me! Help!"

She called back, "What did I tell you, Ross? *Not so loud!*"

My Uncle Herbert from Vermont was mailing an order to his butcher in Boston. First he began the note, "Kindly send two gooses." That didn't seem right, so he started over again with "Kindly send two geeses." Still he wasn't satisfied. He settled his dilemma by writing finally, "Kindly send me a goose." Then he signed his name and added a P. S.: "Send another one with it."

»»✻««

A six-foot-four hunk of man with a five-day growth of beard on his face barged into a Denver saloon, shot out all the lights in the chandelier, tore a telephone directory in half, and then tossed off six straight Scotches without pausing to take breath. Sweeney had never seen anything like it in his twenty years of barkeeping. "I don't reckon I ever seen you around here before," he said admiringly. "Where ya from, stranger?"

The uninvited guest spat squarely into a cuspidor fourteen feet from the bar and growled, "I'm down from Cripple Creek. They threw me out of the mining camp there because I was too effeminate."

»»✻««

Old Moneybags owned half the town, but he looked like an accident on its way to happen. Girls screamed in horror at his touch. Ten in a row refused to marry him despite his wealth. When still another said "no," Moneybags sighed, "You're the eleventh dame to whom I've proposed without avail."

"Try wearing a good thick one next time," she suggested, "and you may get a better break."

(126)

THE INQUIRING REPORTER from *PM* was making the rounds of the cracker-barrel set in a New Hampshire grocery. "Pop," he said to one old codger, "can you remember the first girl you ever kissed?" The old man gave a hollow laugh. "Son," he remarked drily, "I can't even remember the last one."

»»*««

MR. AND MRS. Guinea Pig found themselves surrounded by a pack of 220 snarling dogs and forty-two huntsmen. "If we can only hold out for two hours," said Mr. Guinea Pig optimistically, "we'll outnumber them."

»»*««

MRS. HENNESSY, wife of the town bum, received a note that read, "Leave a thousand dollars under the cottonwood tree in Pizitz Square Tuesday night, or we'll kidnap your husband and you'll never see him again." She answered, "I haven't got any thousand dollars, and I'm counting on you boys to keep your promise."

»»*««

AN ANGUISHED FEMALE voice shrilled over the telephone, "Two young men are trying to get into my room through the window."

"Sorry, lady," was the reply. "You've made a mistake. This isn't Police Headquarters. It's the Fire Department."

"I know that," said the voice impatiently. "It's the Fire Department I'm after. The young men need a bigger ladder."

»»*««

FRESHMAN: Give me a shovel, quick. Percival is stuck in the mud up to his shoetops.

(127)

Sophomore: Why doesn't he walk out?

Freshman: He's in head first.

»»✳««

THE CITY GIRL asked a dairyman why cream was so much more expensive than milk. "It's the cows' fault, ma'am," was the explanation. "They find it much harder to sit on the small bottles."

»»✳««

A LOUD-MOUTHED, showy American tourist had a seat at the finish line of the Oxford-Cambridge crew race that directly adjoined the box reserved for the royal family. While the crowd sat patiently waiting for the race to get under way, some diving boys appeared and everybody began throwing pennies into the river. The American ran out of his English change and ostentatiously threw some $5 gold pieces into the stream. Suddenly a man in livery tapped him on the shoulder. "For the love of heaven, sir," he whispered, "stop throwing those $5 gold pieces. You'll have the King diving."

»»✳««

TEACHER: What do elephants have that no other animals have?

Willie: Little elephants.

»»✳««

A COUNTRY GENTLEMAN with a big valise walked down the railroad track and tapped a busy section hand on the shoulder. "Hey, feller," he asked, "where do I get the Empire State Express?"

"If you don't get off that track," the section hand informed him, "you'll get it square in the behind."

(128)

IT WAS closing time at Kelly's saloon and the same four old drunks were sprawled along the bar. Kelly gathered them up, none too gently, and deposited them in a taxicab outside. "Here's ten bucks," he said. "Drop the guy on the left off at 270 Park Avenue, the one next to him at 20 East 57th Street, the third one at 1112 Park Avenue, and the fourth goes all the way up to Butler Hall in Columbia University." The taxi drove off, but was back again inside of ten minutes.

"Hey, Kelly," cried the driver. "Will you please come over and sort these guys out for me again? I hit a bump on Madison Avenue."

»»*««

THE RESTAURANT PATRON beckoned the waiter. "Please close the window," he said nervously. "I am afraid this steak is going to blow away."

»»*««

IN ONE backward section of the South, certain well-seasoned citizens with no visible means of employment are favored with the complimentary title of Colonel. One of them was called as a witness in a moonshine case and the local lawyer demanded to know exactly how he had come by the title of Colonel. "It's like this," drawled the unperturbed witness. "That Colonel in front of my name is just like the Honorable in front of yours; it don't mean a darn thing."

»»*««

THEY HAD reached the 49th floor of the new skyscraper when Finnegan, the hod carrier, lost his footing and went hurtling off into space. He landed smack on his cranium, went through the cement pavement like a shot, and fetched up in the cellar. His mates came down with a barrel expecting to shovel up the pieces, but there was good old Finnegan rubbing his head and chuckling to himself. "Thank the Good Lord for that concrete pavement," he said. "It broke my fall."

»»*««

A HOUSEPAINTER started working in Mrs. Du Fois' parlor at 9 o'clock one Monday morning. At 9:15 Mrs. Du Fois' roving eye rested admiringly on his magnificent physique, and she suggested that he drop his work for a few moments' chit-chat with her. The painter readily complied with her wishes. At 10:30 the entire process was repeated. When the noon whistle blew, the painter pulled out his lunch and sat back with a contented sigh to enjoy it. At 12:15 Mrs. Du Fois beckoned to him again. The painter shook his head "no" this time, and said very emphatically, "Nothing doing lady. Not on my time."

»»*««

MR. SHLIMOWITZ'S tailor shop was definitely bankrupt. In fact, every stick of furniture in the place had been removed except an old three-legged stool and the telephone, which was scheduled to be yanked out the following morning, Mr. Shlimowitz was aroused from a dark-brown reverie by the insistent ringing of the telephone bell. A hoity-toity voice inquired, "Is this the residence of Mr. J. P. Morgan?"

"Oi," said Mr. Shlimowitz, smiling for the first time in four weeks, "have you got the wrong number!"

»»*««

GUY WILLIAMS, of the Omaha *World Herald*, had his ears pinned back by a nice old lady to whom he had urgently recommended a volume of Shakespeare's plays. "I can't understand why you all make such a fuss over that man," she told him after she had looked over the book. "All he's done is string together a whole lot of very old, well-known quotations."

»»*««

An old tramp sidled up to the back door of a little English tavern called the George and Dragon and beckoned to the landlady. "I ain't had nuthin' to eat for three days," he wheedled. "Would you spare an old man a bite of dinner?"

"I should say not, you good-for-nothing loafer," said the landlady, and slammed the door in his face.

The tramp's face reappeared at the kitchen window. "I was just wonderin'," he said, "if I could 'ave a word or two with George."

»»*««

Mother (*entering room unexpectedly*): Mabel! Get right down from that young man's knee!

Mabel: Nothing doing, Ma. I got here first.

»»*««

When Private Jones left for the South Seas, his girl cried as though her heart would break and vowed that she would be true to him. For two years he carried her image in his heart. Then, one day, he received a curt note which began, "Dear Mr. Jones: I have decided I can't wait for you," she wrote. "The banker's son wants to marry me, and he has already given me a mink coat. Please return my picture."

Jones burned for two days. Then he collected every picture in the camp, including mothers, grandmothers, movie pin-up girls, and naked natives. He sent the whole collection

(131)

to his ex-girl with a penciled note: "I don't remember exactly who you are, but if your picture is among these, please take it out and send the rest back to me."

»»＊««

MOGULL'S FRIENDS convinced him that the Missis was spending too much money. "I'll read her the riot act tonight," swore Mogull. "For the rest of the year she's going to do a little economizing."

The next day they asked him how he had made out. "Great," he said. "I'm giving up poker, liquor, and tobacco."

»»＊««

LEOPOLD GODOWSKI, the famous composer and pianist, was subject to insomnia. His son, who lived with him, was, on the contrary, a very heavy and sound sleeper. It was Godowski Sr.'s amiable habit, when he was having a particularly bad night, to go into his son's room, shake him into reluctant wakefulness, and say, "What's the matter, Leo? Can't you sleep either?"

»»＊««

BILL WOODWARD, the historian, refuses to eat lamb in any form. He insists it has a woolly taste.

»»＊««

A CRANKY old party awoke with a stomachache in the middle of the night and called up his doctor. "I've got a stomachache," he reported.

The doctor was annoyed and said, "Take some bicarbonate of soda. Stop bothering me."

The cranky old party contritely said, "I'm sorry, Doc. I guess it was pretty thoughtless of me to wake you up in the middle of the night for a little thing like a stomachache."

"You didn't wake me," said the doctor sarcastically (making a mental note to send a bill for fifty bucks the next morning). "I had to get up to answer the telephone anyhow."

»»*««

AN EXCITED HOUSEWIFE demanded a personal interview with the postmaster of a big Western city. "Your department is going to pot," she told him. "A week ago my husband left here to complete a big business deal in New York. This morning I received a letter from him, and some idiot in your department post-marked it 'Atlantic City.' "

»»*««

THE CENSUS TAKER asked a hearty mountaineer how many children he had. "Four," was the firm answer, "and, by cricky, that's all I'm going to have too."

"Why so emphatic?" asked the census taker.

"I ain't fergettin' what I read in the Almanac," said the mountaineer. "It said there that every fifth child born is a Chinaman."

»»*««

A MAN who had been on the wagon for two solid years was caught fondling a potent Scotch-and-soda. "I'm just tapering on," he explained.

»»*««

"I THINK you ought to stop taking sleeping pills every night," the doctor told a famous star. "They're habit forming."

"Habit forming!" repeated the star. "Don't be absurd. I've been taking them for twenty years."

"I WOULDN'T DREAM of paying for this picture," the rich matron barked at the portrait painter. "It makes me look just like a gargoyle." "You should have thought of that," said the painter coldly, "before you commissioned it."

IT WAS ALWAYS considered quite the thing for American tourists to inspect the Louvre in Paris, although the knowledge of most of them as far as art was concerned was confined to the Varga girls in *Esquire Magazine*. They tell about one honeymoon couple that pulled up in front of the main entrance. "Tell you what let's do," suggested the husband. "You walk around the inside and I'll walk around the outside and I'll meet you here in twenty minutes."

It is further related that when this couple returned to their home in Chillicothe, somebody asked them, "When you were in Paris, did you se the Mona Lisa?"

"If it was in the Louvre," said the bride firmly, "we seen it."

»»✱««

A JEWELER whose ingenuity exceeded his scruples, bought several thousand dollars' worth of precious stones on credit. He put them all into a coffin, rented a hearse, and headed for Canada with his loot. On the Canadian side of the International Bridge at Niagara Falls a customs inspector stopped him and said, "What's this?"

"Can't you see?" said the dealer. "It's a funeral."

"Funniest funeral I ever saw," said the customs inspector. "Where are the mourners?"

"I'll tell you," said the jeweler. "Some will come in thirty days, some will come in sixty days, and the rest will come in ninety days."

»»✱««

SHIMELHAUSER had been a member of the Happiness Marching and Chowder Club for less than a month when an elimination boxing tournament was announced. The man who had proposed Shimelhauser for membership told him he'd have to enter the tournament to show that he was a good fellow. Shimelhauser had never hit anything in his life except when he wrapped his Chevrolet around a telegraph pole, and he looked forward to his first bout with ill-concealed panic. When he came home after the fight, his wife could see that his worst fears had been realized. He was in terrible shape, and his head was bloody and bowed. "My poor husband," cried Mrs. Shimelhauser, bursting into tears.

"You don't know the worst," gasped Shimelhauser. "They tell me I gotta fight again tomorrow night. I *won*."

»»*««

"It's obvious that that old skinflint isn't going to pay any attention to the bills I sent him," a dentist told his wife one morning. "I'm going up to his house and collect in person."

An hour later he was back, looking very glum. "I can see by your face that he didn't pay you," said his wife.

"He not only didn't pay me," said the dentist ruefully, "but he bit me with my own teeth."

»»*««

Two inmates of the local asylum were sunning themselves on the porch when a farmer drove by with a wagonload of manure. "Hey, farmer," called one of the unfortunates, "what ya gonna do with all that manure?"

"Put it on my strawberries," called back the farmer.

"Hmpff," said the inmate to his friend. "And they call *us* crazy."

»»*««

A conceited author was boasting about his genius to a sour-faced companion who gave no evidence of being impressed. The author in exasperation finally cried, "When Shakespeare is forgotten, they'll remember me."

The companion spoke for the first time. "That's quite true," he said.

»»*««

MRS. MILLER found a note in her husband's coat pocket that read "Jezebel Johnson, Gramercy 7-9999." "You've been holding out on me," she accused her husband. "Exactly who is Jezebel Johnson?"

"Stop jumping to conclusions," said Mr. Miller. "Jezebel Johnson is the name of a race horse. Somebody gave me a tip on her yesterday. The phone number belongs to the bookie who placed my bet for me."

Two days later Mrs. Miller was waiting for her husband when he came home. "You'll be interested to know," she said grimly, "that your race horse called you up a few moments ago."

»»*««

TWO BOY SCOUTS were camping in the woods and were hiding under the blankets to ward off hordes of mosquitoes. One of the kids saw a couple of lightning bugs and said to his companion, "We might as well give up, Tony. Those mosquitoes are out searching for us with lanterns."

»»*««

LOUIS PAUL tells the story of an author who wrote a novel and sent it off to his publisher, only to discover that he had forgotten to put a ribbon in his typewriter. His publisher replied, "We haven't made up our minds yet on your new book, but we will say it is the best manuscript we've seen this week."

(137)

A RED-NOSED GENT, who was obviously four sheets to the wind, sat rocking himself vigorously on a hotel veranda. He appeared to be having quite a discussion with himself, and punctuated this monologue with frequent peals of laughter. Every few minutes, however, he would bring himself up short and mutter a disgusted "phooey." Two men watched his performance with some amusement for a while. One of them finally asked him, "What's going on here, brother?"

"I am telling myself jokes," said the drunk, "and I mush say they are extremely funny."

"Well, then," said the other, "what's the idea of those violent 'phooeys' every now and then?"

"That," said the drunk with some dignity," is when I tell myself a joke I have heard before."

»» * ««

THE GREATEST OPTIMIST in Kincaid County was the elder Schultz boy; his young brother, on the other hand, was a confirmed pessimist. Their Christmas presents were laid out under the same tree. The pessimist got three cases of twenty-year-old Scotch. "Dunnervetter," he groaned, "am I going to have an awful hangover!"

The optimist got a bag of fertilizer. "Goody, goody," said he. "Somebody has given me a horse!"

»» * ««

THE *Daily Blast* gave Wilkins, Jr., a job as reporter for the very excellent reason that Wilkins, Sr., was its biggest advertising account. Young Wilkins' first assignment was to cover the most important society wedding the town had had in twenty years. Late that evening the editor found Wilkins with his feet on the desk reading the comic strips. "Where's that wedding story I sent you for?" demanded the editor.

"I'm sorry, sir," said Wilkins. "It turns out there is no story. The bridegroom ran away last night with some strip-tease artist, so they had to call off the whole wedding."

»»✳««

"MY SPONSOR threw me a big dinner last night," confided Milton Berle, "but it didn't hit me."

»»✳««

MR. MACCLAREN climbed onto the Riverside Drive bus trailing a heavy suitcase behind him. He handed the conductor a nickel and waxed very indignant when the conductor informed him that the fare on the Riverside Drive line was a dime. After a heated exchange, the conductor lost his temper completely. First he threw Mr. MacClaren off the bus, and then he picked up Mr. MacClaren's suitcase and flung it over the parapet into the Hudson River below. Mr. Mac-Claren shook his fist after the disappearing bus and shrieked in a rage, "It's not enough that you tried to murder me in cold blood, you dirrrrty dog, but you've drowned me son Jock."

»»✳««

ED WYNN tells a story about the man who was driving with his wife in the midst of a violent rainstorm. She was bawling him out unmercifully when suddenly, to his delighted surprise, she stopped talking entirely and sat silently shaking her head vigorously from left to right. He didn't want to question his luck, so he drove through the rain for half an hour peering straight ahead. Then he looked over and found out the cause of it all. His wife's nose had gotten caught in the windshield wiper.

(139)

It HADN'T snowed in a certain Southern metropolis for twenty years, but this particular evening the city was blanketed in white, and Clancy experienced a sudden desire to go for a sleigh ride. "If I only had a sleigh," he told his wife, "what a wonderful time I'd have tonight, begad."

"Your friend Milligan has a sleigh," his wife reminded him. "I'm sure he'd be glad to loan it to you."

"A great idea," agreed Clancy. "I know Milligan will let me have it. I'll go and ask him."

The path to Milligan's house, unfortunately, was studded with saloons, and Clancy felt it his duty to bestow patronage on each one. After the first saloon, he was still in a rather happy mood, and said to himself, "I *hope* Milligan will loan me that sleigh, but maybe he will be afraid I'll smash it up."

After his second stop, he was feeling slightly more belligerent. "It will be a dirty trick of Milligan if he won't let me take that sleigh when he isn't using it himself."

He told the third bartender, "If Milligan doesn't let me use that sleigh, by all that's holy, I will never talk to the rapscallion again."

After his twelfth drink Clancy was really spoiling for a fight. He pulled up in front of Milligan's house about 2:30 A.M., picked up a stone and sent it crashing through Milligan's bedroom window. A moment later Milligan, purple with rage, appeared at the broken window. "What son of Satan threw that stone?" he demanded.

"I did," cried Clancy, shaking his fist. "And what's more, you can take that blank-blank sleigh of yours, ye stingy old blank, and shove it down your throat."

(140)

A CONFIRMED woman-hater looked up from the piece of wood he was whittling by the old cracker barrel. "Women wouldn't be here except for a little misunderstanding," he snarled. "The Lord came down from the sky one day and asked Adam how things were going. Adam felt a little pernickety that day and he said, 'Lord, you ain't givin' me no company.' 'That's right,' said the Lord. 'Maybe what you need is a nice woman.' Adam turned white at that and said, 'Aw, Lord, can't you take a rib?' Well, sir, that's just what the Lord did. The next day Eve put in an appearance and you fellers know the rest of the terrible story."

»» * ««

HERE'S A NOTICE that was pasted on the bullentin board of a Texas airport: "The following enlisted men will pick up their good-conduct medals at the Supply Room this afternoon. Failure to comply with this order will result in disciplinary action."

»» * ««

WHEN MR. BERNSTEIN dropped dead in his office, it was the sad duty of the accountant, Mr. Harper, to break the doleful tidings to his widow. He found Mrs. Bernstein lapping up a hefty plate of borscht soup. "Mrs. Bernstein," said Harper with an apologetic sigh. "I am sorry to tell you that your husband just dropped dead."

Mrs. Bernstein whirled on him and shook a soup spoon in his face. "I heard you, all right, young man," she informed him. "And just as soon as I finish this borscht soup, are you going to hear a woman have hysterics!"

(141)

FARMER HIGGINS was showing his poultry ranch to a fascinated young city dweller. "How do you manage to tell the ganders from the geese?" she asked.

"I don't do too much worrying about that," explained the farmer. "I just turn them all out together and let 'em figure it out for themselves."

»»*««

"I COOKED a spoonge cake for you, darling," said the young bride, puckering for a kiss, "but it didn't turn out right. I think the grocer sent me the wrong kind of sponges."

»»*««

THE KEEPER found little Mr. Snoop very easy to satisfy. Mr. Snoop rather fancied himself as an Izaak Walton. The keeper simply perched him on top of a ladder, at the foot of which he set an empty pail. Mr. Snoop would sit happily for hours dangling a string in and out of the pail. One day another keeper sauntered by. "Catch anything?" he inquired pleasantly.

"Don't be a loon," said Snoop indignantly. "How can you catch anything by dangling a piece of string in an empty kitchen pail?"

»»*««

A HILLBILLY and his bride came to Pittsburgh for their honeymoon and bought tickets for the performance of a touring musical show. At the end of the first act, the hillbilly presented himself at the box office and paid $1.40 extra to have his seats changed from the balcony to the orchestra floor. Ten minutes after the second act started, he was back at the box office. "Give me our money back," he demanded. "That's the same bum show that's playing upstairs."

(142)

LINSCOTT WAS passing out cigars. He announced that he had just received a bundle from heaven. "Boy or girl?" asked an adoring secretary.

"Neither," beamed Linscott. "It was my laundry."

»»✳««

AN ENGLISHMAN spent a hectic fortnight in America. He never did manage to get himself straightened out on the names and uses of American currency. "It was perfectly amazing how quickly I got used to American ways," he told his friends when he got back to London. "Take those bally American coins and bills, for instance. When I got out of a taxi, I just thrust all the American money I had at the driver and let him figure out the correct amount. Do you know, I was absolutely right every time. It took just what I had—to the last penny."

»»✳««

JOHN STRALEY recalls a town meeting in Minnesota where the subject of discussion was a proposed bridge over the local creek. The estimated cost was $50,000 and a small clique was determined to railroad the proposition through. No opposition was encountered until suddenly Ole Olsen, a frugal citizen, horrified at the size and apparent uselessness of the project, leaped to his feet. "Dat is vun awful vaste," he shouted. "For a bridge over dat creek—fifty t'ousand dollar? Vy, it ain't worth nutting. I can spit half vay across dat creek."

The chairman of the meeting banged down his gavel. "Mr. Olsen," he roared, "you are out of order."

"Dot is right," answered Ole in a bellow that shook the building. "If I vasn't out of order—I could spit all d' vay across."

Rex Stout, bewhiskered creator of the fabulous detective, Nero Wolf, was a passenger aboard a crowded Madison Avenue bus one day. An aggressive little man battled his way to Stout's side and, unable to reach a strap, forthwith clutched a strand of the author's beard in a grip of iron. Stout spluttered indignantly for a full block and finally demanded, "will you kindly take your paws away from my beard?"

"What's the matter, mister?" said the little man. "Are you getting off?"

THE OFFICE BEAUTY was regaling her bored companions with the tale of her adventures on the previous night. "This feller," she said, "took me up to his apartment and showed me a closet that contained at least fifteen absolutely perfect mink coats. And what do you know," she said, "he *gave* me one of them."

"What did you have to do?" asked the skeptic in the audience.

"Just shorten the sleeves," she said.

»»*««

A FARMER took his young son to the County Fair. The boy watched the proceedings with great interest; finally he turned to his father and asked, "Why does that man go around patting and pinching the cows?"

"He's doing that," said the father, "because he wants to buy a cow and is trying to make sure that he will get good meat."

A few days later, the boy excitedly called to his father. "Hurry, hurry, papa! The letter carrier is buying our cook!"

»»*««

ON HIS WAY to California, Harper noticed an Indian brave lolling indolently on a Santa Fe station platform. An efficiency expert to the last, Harper braced him with, "Chief, why don't you get yourself a job?" "Why?" countered the Indian pleasantly. "Well," said Harper, slightly nettled, "you get a job and pile up a bank account for yourself. Wouldn't you like that?" "Why?" said the Indian again. "So you can retire," shouted Harper, "and never have to work again!" "I'm not working now," pointed out the Indian.

(145)

AN ARMY CHAPLAIN aboard a troop train was in obvious distress, and a colored corporal came over to ask if there was anything he could do to help him. "I'll be all right," said the chaplain carefully. "They gave me three shots this morning and it sort of knocked me out."

"I sho' understand," commiserated the corporal. "Three shots of the stuff they sells around this state would knock anybody out."

»»＊««

"I MADE my husband a marble cake," pouted Mrs. Falk, "and when I offered him a piece, he said, 'I'll take it for granite.' "

»»＊««

LITTLE MARY'S MOTHER and father both fancied themselves as violinists. In front of both of them a visitor asked Mary, "Who do you think plays better, your mother or your father?"

Mary, who will probably end up in the diplomatic corps, answered, "Heifetz."

»»＊««

MINISTER: Is your grandfather at home?

Junior: I ain't seen him.

Minister: You *haven't* seen him. Where's your grammar?

Junior: In the kitchen making up to the iceman.

»»＊««

AT A RECENT meeting of the Twentieth Century Benevolent Association, Mr. Wolf delivered an impassioned speech on the subject of the steadily dwindling attendance. "The reason is," he said, "that our meeting hall is always dirty: the chairs are never dusted; everyone who uses it throws cigar butts and cigarette stubs on the floors. Mr. Chairman, what we need here is a cuspidor!"

(146)

In a corner of the hall sat Mr. Hirsch, a quiet little man who, in all his twenty years of regular attendance, had never lifted his voice to criticize, praise or suggest. Mr. Wolf's statements, however, moved him deeply, and he waved his hand for attention. Surprised at this unexpected activity, the chairman immediately gave him the floor, and Mr. Hirsch addressed the membership.

"Mr. President, Mr. Vice-President, Mr. Secretare, Mr. Chairman, Mr. Soggint-at-Arms, and fellow members. For twenty years I have been coming reglar to meetings, but I never been any kind of an officer. How about making *me* that Cuspidor?"

»»✳««

A VERY agitated lady got her doctor on the telephone. "Come quick," she cried. "My ten-year-old boy just swallowed a fountain pen." The doctor remained calm. "I will get over as soon as I can," he said, "but there are several patients in the office now and you may not see me for three or four hours."

"Three or four hours," echoed the lady. "What will I do in the meantime?"

"I am afraid you will have to use a pencil," said the doctor.

»»✳««

A LONG ISLAND potato married an Idaho potato, and eventually they had a little sweet potato. The little one flourished, and in due time announced to its parents that it wanted to marry Lowell Thomas. "But you can't marry Lowell Thomas," declared the parents. "He's just a commentator."

»»✳««

LONDON *Tit-Bits* tells of a thrifty native who discovered that instead of putting coins in the gas meter, he could obtain

(147)

much the same effect by blowing smartly into the slot. At length an inspector from the gas company called to read the meter. He was obviously puzzled by his findings. "What's the matter?" asked the householder.

"Man," said the inspector. "I don't understand it at all. The company seems to owe you three pounds ha'penny."

»»*««

DELANCEY STREET was blanketed with snow, and the wind was howling from the west. Suddenly one of the peddlars began yelling, "Hitler, Hitler."

A cop came up, watched the peddlar for a minute, scratched his head and asked, "What are you shouting 'Hitler for?"

"If I yell 'bananas'," answered the peddlar, "who would come out on a day like this?"

»»*««

MR. MCGLOMBIE and his wife had always wanted a ride in a plane, but McGlombie turned white when he heard the tariff for a taxi-ride in the air. It was $20. The amused pilot said, "I will make you a proposition, Mr. McGlombie. You and your wife get in and I will give you a ride for half an hour. If you don't say a single word while we are up, I will only charge you $5."

Mr. McGlombie thought this was a fair proposal and he and his wife climbed into the plane. The pilot thereupon took them on the wildest half hour's ride that could possibly be imagined, looping the loop, riding upside down, and going through dizzying dives and tailspins. Finally he set his craft down on the ground.

"I've got to hand it to you. Mr. McGlombie," said the

pilot. "It took guts to go through all that without uttering a sound."

"Aye," said McGlombie, mopping his brow with his handkerchief. "But ya'll never know how close I came to talkin' when the wife fell out."

»» * ««

Two IRISHMEN, newly arrived in America, decided to try their luck in one of our restaurants. The waiter brought them their food, at the same time placing a dish of horseradish on the table. Neither Clancy nor Patrick had ever seen horseradish before, and to them it looked like a new kind of jelly. Clancy decided to try it, and took a heaping mouthful. Immediately the tears sprang to his eyes.

"What's the matter, Clancy? Why are you crying?"

Clancy didn't want to admit his mistake, and replied: "I am crying because I just thought of my poor grandfather who was hung."

Patrick sympathized, and then decided to try the horseradish himself. In no time at all he too was crying.

Now it was Clancy's turn to ask the reason for the tears.

"I'm crying," said Patrick, "because they didn't hang you at the same time they hung your grandfather."

»» * ««

A LAWYER listened very attentively while the prospective client gave details of the case. "You can't lose," said the lawyer finally. "If that case is presented properly, any jury in the land will deliver a verdict inside of ten minutes. Hand over a $100 retainer and I will handle the case for you."

"No, thanks," said the client. "I don't think I'll pursue the matter further. I was giving you the other fellow's side."

(149)

LENKOWSKY POINTED to a platter in the showcase. "A quarter's worth from dot meat," he ordered. "You mean the ham?" asked the delicatessen man. "Who asked vot it vas?" countered Lenkowsky.

»»✳««

THE JUDGE looked very severe. "Mr. Acropolous," he said, "your wife says you hit her over the head with a baseball bat and threw her down a flight of stairs. What have you got to say for yourself?"

Mr. Acropolous rubbed the side of his nose with his hand and meditated. Finally he said, "Your Honor, I guess there are three sides to this case: my wife's story, my story and the truth."

»»✳««

MR. JONES was visibly undone as he staggered into the locker room. "What's the matter, old boy?" asked the pro sympathetically.

"I just killed my wife, that's what's the matter," said Mr. Jones.

"Good God, how did you do that?"

"I was over on the practice tee and didn't see her coming up behind me. I took a back swing and hit her on the head. She dropped dead."

"That's tough," said the pro. "What club were you using?"

"The niblick," said Mr. Jones.

"That's the club," said the pro.

»»✳««

MR. MAYES shook his head wonderingly. "Just look at this suit I am wearing," he observed. "The wool was grown in

(150)

Australia, the cloth was woven in New England, and the thread comes from India. The suit was made in Baltimore and I bought it in Buenos Aires."

"What's so remarkable about that?" asked his friend.

"Isn't it wonderful," mused Mayes, ignoring the interruption, "that so many people can make a living out of something I haven't paid for?"

»»✳«««

A MAN was having a facial massage in his neighborhood barber shop. The barber had just draped a very hot towel around his countenance when a lad tore into the shop, crying, "Mr. Wilkins, Mr. Wilkins, your house is burning down." The man grunted with dismay, pulled the hot towel off his face, and went charging madly after the boy without even stopping to pick up his coat, collar and tie. After puffing his way through three or four crowded blocks, he suddenly stopped short and demanded, "What on earth am I running this way for? My name isn't Wilkins."

»»✳«««

THE LATE Stephen Leacock liked to sing the praises of the country boys of Vermont. "You have no idea how strong they are," he wrote. "When a farm wagon is stuck in the mud, it's nothing to see one of them walk up behind the vehicle and, with a mighty heave, easily break a shoulder blade."

»»✳«««

"FOR WHAT was Louis XIV chiefly responsible?" asked the history professor.

The eager beaver in the front row had his hand up in a jiffy. "Louis XV, sir," he replied.

A HARLEM DEACON felt that his flock was not sufficiently terrorized by his predecessor's description of Hell, so he set about remedying this situation. "Brethren," he demanded. "Has none of you seed molten lead pourin' an' sizzlin' out of a furnace?" A few brethren said they had. "Sisters an' brothers," the deacon assured them. "In de place I'se tellin' you 'about, dey uses dat stuff fo' shaved ice."

»»✳««

MRS. BERNBAUM came uptown for her first symphony concert at Carnegie Hall. Her neighbors heard nothing else the next afternoon. "Such an experience," she sighed blissfully.

Her friend asked her which piece she had enjoyed the best.

"Let me see now," she mused. "I guess bast I liked Tchaikowsky's Symphony—if you'll pardon the expression—No. 2."

»»✳««

SEVERAL DAYS after his father died, little Johnny was stopped on the street by a neighbor. "And what were your poor father's last words?" the neighbor asked.

"He didn't have any," Johnny answered. "Mama was with him to the very end."

»»✳««

A DILAPIDATED RAGAMUFFIN horrified members of one of the swankiest golf clubs on Long Island by suddenly appearing on the first tee munching a very dirty-looking ham sandwich. The chairman of the greens committee angrily bade him be on his way, but the interloper just stared at him and went on nibbling his sandwich. Several other members came up and grew increasingly indignant when the man ignored

their command to depart. Finally the chairman could stand it no longer. He fastened one hand about the little man's neck, the other on the seat of his pants, and threw him clean over the hedge into the public highway that adjoins the Club property. The ragamuffin picked himself up gingerly and spoke for the first time: "That's a hell of a way to get new members!"

»»*««

A POOL CHAMPION stared so hard at a bald-headed gentleman that the latter bridled and demanded, "Have you never seen a bald-headed man before?" "Don't get sore," said the champ. "It's just that I could have sworn I put you in a side-pocket last night."

»»*««

EXTRACT FROM a Wall Street broker's petty cash book:

April 1.	Advertisement for pretty secretary	$1.60
3.	Violets	.75
4.	Candy	1.25
8.	Secretary's salary	30.00
10.	Flowers	3.00
11.	Candy for wife	7.50
15.	Secretary's salary	40.00
18.	Hand-bag	12.50
19.	Candy for wife	3.00
22.	Gloria's salary	60.00
24.	Theatre and dinner, Gloria and self	55.00
25.	Chocolates for wife	.90
28.	Fur coat for wife	1800.00
29.	Advertisement for male secretary	1.60

(153)

In Hollywood no script is considered worthy unless it has been rewritten at least six times. They even rewrite Shakespeare and the Bible. Lincoln Barnett tells about a scenario writer named Cyril who lay dying. On his deathbed he composed a poem and asked his closest pal to read it at his funeral. After his death the friend called another writer and said, "You gotta come and help me. Cyril gave me a poem to read at his grave, and frankly, it stinks. I want you to help me fix it up."

So the two friends completely rewrote the deceased's last words.

»»✳««

In the middle of his lunch a man noticed the clock behind the counter and made a dive for his hat and coat. "Two o'clock," he cried. "I've got to get down to Gimbel's. My wife is supposed to meet me there at one o'clock sharp, and I don't want to be late."

»»✳««

The salesman was having a tough time selling Mr. Levi a dictograph. "Think of the time it will save you. Instead of waiting for your secretary to come in every time you want to write a letter, you just dictate into this machine. Whenever you have a free moment, the dictograph is ready and waiting for you."

Levi was unimpressed. In despair, the salesman brought forth his final suggestion. "Let me install one of these machines for a week, without cost to you. If, at the end of that time, it hasn't done everything I said it would, I'll take it out again."

Mr. Levi agreed, and at the end of the week the salesman came back. As soon as he came in, Mr. Levi screamed at him,

"Take dis machine out frum mine office. Take it out qvick."

The salesman was taken aback. "What's the matter? Didn't it do everything I promised?"

"Yes, it did everytink you said," conceded Mr. Levi. "But did you ever hear mit vot an eccent it speaks?"

»»✳««

EARL WILSON, the *Post's* famous saloon editor, wrote a radio script for a famous comedian. The comedian listened to it without cracking a single smile. "Okay, okay," pouted Wilson. "They laughed at other innovators—Robert Fulton, Alexander Graham Bell, Thomas Edison . . ." "They did?" said the comedian. "Who wrote their programs?"

»»✳««

OUTSIDE A MONASTERY in Tibet, two venerable lamas sunned themselves day after day, rarely talking, engaged in deep meditation. On February 14th, one lama stopped stroking his beard long enough to remark, "Life, my friend, is like a well." The other said nothing until March 9th, when he suddenly rumbled, "Why is life like a well?" On April 22d, the first lama shrugged his shoulders and commented, "All right, have it your way. Life *isn't* like a well."

»»✳««

THE TOWN DRUNK tried to get to bed without disturbing his wife, but heard her coming downstairs the moment he shut the door. He made a dive for the library, reached for a book, and was sitting under the lamp when his wife barged into the room. "Hello, darling," he said disarmingly "I thought I'd read a little tonight."

"You did, did you?" said she coldly. "Well, you just shut that valise and come up to bed."

(155)

THE MAN in lower six was snoring lustily. The lady in the next berth tapped on the partition, but he didn't hear her. Finally she banged so loudly that she almost tore it down altogether. Awake at last, the man rubbed his eyes and grumbled surlily, "Nothing doing, lady. I seen you get on."

»»*««

A CUB REPORTER in Iowa reported that a local farmer had been robbed of 2,025 pigs. The cagey night editor thought the figure pretty high and phoned the farmer to check up. "Is it true that you lost two thousand twenty-five pigs?"

"Yeth," sighed the farmer.

The cagey editor thanked him and changed the copy to make the loss read, "two sows and twenty-five pigs."

»»*««

THE LATE Justice Cardozo was a bad sailor. A friend found him leaning far over the rail of the *Aquitania* in midocean one day and, in a concerned voice, asked, "Can't I do something for you, Judge?"

"You certainly can," said the Justice. "Overrule this motion."

»»*««

THE PRESENCE of a lot of cocky and hard-bitten American aviators in Russian bases had some strange effects on the earnest efforts of some Russians who were studying the English language. One Russian private approached an American Colonel, gave him a snappy salute and exclaimed, "Good morning, jerk."

»»*««

AMERICAN TOURISTS, brought up on the black, glaring headlines of United States newspapers, always find it a bit dif-

(156)

ficult to adjust themselves to the terse, conservative story heads in the English press. One New Yorker, for instance, chanced to be in Waterloo Station the day that an engineer fell asleep at the throttle of his cab. The engineer's train hurtled into the terminal at sixty miles an hour and scattered death and debris in all directions. Over sixty persons were killed, and hundreds seriously injured. The next morning the New Yorker hurried to read the story in the London *Times*. He found it on page seven under the headline, "Mishap in Waterloo."

The densest fog in fifty years once cut off England for three days from all communication with the outside world. The London *Mail's* headline will never be forgotten by journalists: "Heavy Fog; Entire Continent Isolated."

»»✳««

COLLECTING BILLS from delinquent accounts is getting to be as hazardous a vocation as washing windows on the 96th floor of the Empire State Building. Here are two classic letters one expert on such matters received from evasive debtors:

Exhibit 1:

"Dear Sir: I have your collection letter of the 13th, and am happy to give you the following information. We have divided our creditors into three groups:

Class A: Those who will be paid promptly.

Class B: Those who will be paid some time.

Class C: Those who will never be paid.

In consideration of the friendly tone of your letter we are promoting you from Class C to Class B."

Exhibit 2:

"I don't like the insistent tone of your last letter. Every

month we put all our bills into an old sombrero, and my wife, blind-folded, picks out one of them. The lucky one that's chosen gets paid. Unless you stop sending us those snooty letters, come next month we won't even put your bill in the hat."

»»*««

DURING A RECENT near-hurricane in New York, Marshall Best of the Viking Press looked out of his window and remarked, "It's raining cats and dogs today." "I know," said his partner, Ben Huebsch, an incurable punster. "I just stepped into a poodle."

»»*««

MRS. RIFKIND turned to her dinner guest and beamed, "Mr. Shlophannes, I know how you love blintzes. Why don't you take a couple more?" Mr. Shlophannes blushed happily. "I would love to take some more, Mrs. Rifkind," he said, "but I am positively embarrassed. I have already had eight." "You've already had eleven," corrected Mrs. Rifkind, "but who counts around here?"

»»*««

A LITTLE old lady came up to a train announcer at Grand Central and said, "Young man, where do I catch my train?"

"That depends on where you're going," said the announcer pleasantly.

"You're very impertinent," snapped the old lady. "What business is it of yours where I am going? But if you must know, I am bound for Boston."

The announcer obligingly picked up her three bags, found her a seat in the Boston coach, and put the bags on the rack above her head. As he descended to the platform, the old lady leaned out the window and cackled at him. "I guess I fooled you, you impertinent young man. I'm really going to Buffalo."

»»✻««

FLANAGAN BUMPED into his friend Dooley just outside the Whoops-a-Daisy bar. Both gentlemen were listing slightly to leeward and had a fine aroma on their breaths. "Flanagan, me boy," said Dooley, "you're just in time to come to McGrath's wake with me."

"A fine idea that," allowed Flanagan. "But I never had the pleasure of your friend McGrath's acquaintance."

Dooley assured Flanagan that this made no difference whatever, and the two men reeled into McGrath's homestead, where a first-class wake was hitting on all cylinders. Flanagan just made the grand piano in the front parlor when his legs gave way beneath him. As he sank down, his jaw gave the ivory keys of the piano a terrific jolt. He looked at them wonderingly, then turned to his friend Dooley, and said in tones of soft admiration, "It is true that I never saw McGrath in rale life, but I must say he sure had a fine set of teeth."

»»✻««

A HARASSED Washington official regarded the latest entrant to his office wearily. "Good morning, Mr. er-er-Simpson," he said. "I presume you brought a sample of the merchandise you are trying to sell the Government."

"Hardly," said Mr. Simpson. "You may recall that it was you who asked me to call to see you and that I am a builder of suspension bridges."

(159)

FERGUSON WAS driving his girl through the park one hot summer night when they passed a popcorn stand. "Yum," said the girl. "That popcorn sure smells good."

"Wait a minute," said Ferguson generously, "and I will drive up closer so you can get a better whiff of it."

»»*««

YOU'VE PROBABLY heard the one about the lady who had water on the knee. She got rid of it by wearing pumps.

And it must have been her father who suffered from water on the brain. One cold night he fell asleep and the water froze. When he awoke, he couldn't remember a thing. Everything had slipped his mind.

»»*««

"I DIDN'T have no part in the fight, Your Honor," swore Rastus solemnly on the witness stand. "Just as soon as I seen there was trouble I started runnin' as fast as I could. Then I heard two shots ring out."

"Two shots?" interrupted the judge. "The last witness said there was only one shot fired."

"Oh, no, sir," insisted Rastus. "I counted two shots definitely—one when the bullet passed me and the other when I passed the bullet."

»»*««

AN AMERICAN in London was having a terrible time with his pronunciation. It was bad enough to learn that Worcester was pronounced "Wooster," and that Chumley was spelled out as Cholmondeley. Then he saw a marquee on a picture house. It read, "A REVIVAL OF CAVALCADE: PRONOUNCED SUCCESS."

"That settles it," said the American. "I'm going home."

(160)

THE LINKS were very crowded one Sunday and there was a long wait at the second tee for every foursome. Suddenly a lone player, came up and nervously addressed three foursomes that were waiting their turn. "Gentlemen," he said, "I beg you to let me play through."

"You must be crazy," said a member of one of the foursomes. "You know very well that a single player has no rights here on Sunday."

"I know," agreed the lone golfer, "and ordinarily I wouldn't make such a request, but I just had bad news from home. The doctor phoned to tell me that my wife is dying."

»»✳««

TROUBLE BREWED in San Francisco's Chinatown recently, and one Hop Sung Lee was earmarked for liquidation. The bullet, unfortunately, clipped an innocent bystander, Willie Lee. The following morning Willie's widow received a note: "Please excuse. Mere slip of tong."

»»✳««

A NOTED San Francisco bookseller, in his cups and in a hurry to get home to his deserted bride in Oakland, spied a ferry about fifteen feet from the Market Street slip. He made a magnificent running broad jump and landed on the deck like Balaam coming through Jerusalem. Pulling himself together, he hiccuped and exulted, "Hot diggety, I made it, didn't it?"

"You certainly did," agreed a bystander. "But why didn't you wait? The ferry was just coming in."

»»✳««

A GAMBLER's seven-year-old son, asked to count in school, responded promptly, "1, 2, 3, 4, 5, 6, 7, 8, 9, 10, Jack, Queen, King."

A YOUNG MAN stopped into a clothing store to ask the price of a suit on display in the window. "You picked the best suit in the place," said the merchant approvingly, "and to show you that I like to do business with a man who has such good taste, I am going to make you a special proposition. I wouldn't ask you $62 for the suit. I wouldn't ask you $52. I wouldn't ask you $42. $32 is my price for you, my friend."

The customer replied, "I wouldn't give you $32 and I wouldn't give you $22. My offer is $12."

"Sold," said the merchant. "That's the way I like to do business. No chiseling."

»»✻««

THE HOLLYWOOD agent said at lunch, "My wife says she is going to leave me if I don't stop running around."

"Too bad," said his friend.

"Yes, it is," said the agent. "I'm going to miss her."

»»✻««

A MAN was on his way home on a blustery January night when he saw in the window of a de-luxe fruit shop a basket of beautiful ripe peaches. Thinking how pleased and surprised his wife would be with such an unseasonable gift, he entered the shop and asked the price of the peaches. The lady behind the counter informed him loftily that they were $12 a dozen. The man was staggered, mumbled, "Thank you," and moved in something of a daze toward the door. Suddenly he was back in front of the haughty saleslady, planking a fifty-cent piece on the counter. "What's that for?" she inquired.

"Pardon me, madam," he said meekly, "I stepped on a grape."

(162)

THE SHARECROPPER sold his season's yield for $40. The purchaser counted out four $10 bills and said, "Mose, I will wrap them up for you." After supper that night, the sharecropper lovingly turned to his precious package. When he opened it, however, he found only three bills. For a long time he looked at them sadly and then he shook his head and said, "They's tricks in all trades, but Ah reckon Ah'd ruther be a good money wropper than mos' anything."

»»*««

A FLY-BY-NIGHT columnist chiseled his way into a swank party hosted by one of America's leading and wittiest actresses. When he left, he gave her a limp hand and said, "Thanks for the swell party."

"That's quite okay," said the actress. "Do remind me to invite you the next time."

»»*««

SHOLEM ASCH tells a story about an impoverished cobbler who lived in a tiny village in Europe and had an incredibly ugly daughter. He had long abandoned any hope of ever getting her off his hands, when one day the local matchmaker dropped this bombshell: "I have a match for your daughter." "It can't be," the cobbler exclaimed. "Not after all these years. Who is the man?" "Count Petrovsky," calmly announced the matchmaker.

The father was stunned. Count Petrovsky, the richest, the most aristocratic, the most handsome—no, he couldn't permit it. "My daughter would only be unhappy," he said. "She wouldn't know how to act in his company. The Count is out of her class."

The matchmaker pleaded, pointed out that the cobbler

(163)

was standing in the way of his daughter's happiness—but to no avail. The best he could do was persuade the bewildered man to submit the matter to the wise old mayor. This he did, and, after much discussion and meditation on the part of the mayor, was told that the matter had best be referred to the governor. Again much discussion and much thought, and the governor said "Yes." The matchmaker snatched up his coat and ran from the room. The cobbler dashed after him, grabbed him by the sleeve, and asked, "Where are you going?" "Now," replied the matchmaker, "all I have to do is sell the idea to Count Petrovsky."

»»*««

A LADY, shopping at a local fish market, poked her finger into a succulent flounder and asked, "How much is this fish?"

"Seventy cents," answered the merchant.

"How much does it weigh?" she asked.

"I haven't the faintest idea," said the fish man, "but it will cost you seventy cents."

"Haven't you got a scale?" persisted the shopper.

"Lady," said the fish man, "I don't sell any scales. You gotta buy the whole fish."

»»*««

LELA ROGERS, Ginger's mother, opened a small playhouse in Hollywood to present budding actors and playwrights to cinema big-wigs in a professional way. One particularly shy and awkward young man presented himself. "What's your name?" she asked. "Ed Edon," he said. Seeking to put him more at ease, she commented, "That's a very euphonious name." "Oh, no, ma'am," he assured her. "It's my own."

(164)

IN THE EARLY 1930S, a reporter on the *Paris-Herald* got completely fed up with sappy press handouts about the comings and goings of royalty and society bigwigs and slipped the following into print when nobody was looking:

"The Prince of Wales visited the children's section of the British hospital yesterday. He smiled graciously at all the little girls and boys there, but one little boy did not appreciate the favor of the Prince's visit.

"The Prince went up to the little boy and said, 'Little boy, what is your name?'

"The little boy said, 'What business is it of yours?'

"That was not very polite and it made the Prince very angry. It made him so darn angry, in fact, that he took his cane and bashed the little boy's brain out."

The end of the story is that the reporter, of course, was fired. Shed a tear or two for unrewarded genius!

»»*««

A CAROLINA mountaineer cornered a young sprout one evening and demanded. "See here. You been a courtin' my daughter for three years. You got to tell me about your intentions. Be they honorable or dishonorable?"

The young sprout's face brightened visibly. "You mean I got a choice?" he asked.

»»*««

TWO SCOTSMEN played sixteen holes of golf without saying a word to each other. On the seventeenth tee, McDougall broke the long silence. "I am one up," he announced.

The other looked at him with unmitigated disgust. "Chatterbox," he rasped.

(165)

AN EMBITTERED AUTHOR summed up his publisher as follows: "Broke as the Ten Commandments, so conceited that he does crossword puzzles with a fountain pen, and so crooked that every time I shake hands with him I count my fingers."

»»*««

THE ROMANCE between Gloria and Walter was a typical summer-resort affair—two weeks of a whirlwind courtship that ended when Gloria had to take the bus back to New York and Macy's basement. It was their last tête-à-tête. "Gloria," said Walter, "you're a wonderful girl, but if you don't mind my saying so, you don't take full advantage of your natural gifts. Now, here's what I want you to do. Just as soon as you get back to New York, you go into Jaeckel's and order yourself a beautiful mink coat. Then go over to Bergdorf-Goodman and have a couple of $200 suits made to order for you. There is something about an expensive suit that a connoisseur can tell three blocks away. Then you go to Tiffany's and get a few solid-gold clips and a real diamond bracelet. You're too beautiful to wear that cheap costume jewelry. Top it all off with a few sprays of orchids from Schling's, and then you'll really be something."

Gloria's eyes rolled with delight. "What wonderful suggestions, Walter!" she breathed. "But after I've got all these things, how can I get in touch with you?"

"Oh, just call me," said Walter, "at Wadsworth 6–9277."

"Is that your home or your business telephone?" asked Gloria.

"It's the candy store at the corner," said Walter. "But they always call me."

(166)

THERE WAS a loud knock on Mrs. Murphy's door. When she opened it, the red-faced party demanded, "Be you the Widow Murphy?"

"I am Mrs. Murphy," said she indignantly, "but I be no widow."

"You be'n't, eh?" cackled the visitor. "Wait till you see what they're bringing upstairs."

»»*««

A WISP of a man bought a ferocious tiger at an auction sale, outbidding several prominent circus proprietors. "What on earth are you going to do with that man-eating beast?" he was asked by the head of a wild-animal act. "Going into competition with us?"

"Oh, no," said the little man. "It isn't that. But my poor wife died last week and I'm lonely."

»»*««

A MAN who sports a set of whiskers these days has to take a lot of abuse from the so-called wits with whom he associates. Let's consider for instance, the case of Monty Woolley, sometimes known as "The Beard." Mr. Woolley is pretty sick of alleged humor concerning his hirsute adornment. Fred Allen, for instance, informed him that he looked like a cross between a sofa with the lining showing through and a man who swallowed a St. Bernard dog and left his tail hanging out. Earl Wilson yodeled, "Hey, Monty, why don't you put some hollandaise on that broccoli?" A drunk at the Stork Club capped the climax by piping, "Say, Schnauzer, what are you doing with that muff?" "Earning considerably more money than you are," answered the outraged Mr. Woolley.

(167)

JOE FAYE bought a book that was guaranteed to cure stuttering. "It t-t-taught me to s-s-say 'Peter Piper picked a peck of pickled peppers,'" mourned Faye, "but the t-t-trouble is, that expression comes up so s-s-seldom in conversation."

»»✳««

THE LOS ANGELES Limited wasn't ten minutes out of the Chicago Union Station when a sweet little old lady noticed a man in the front of the car whose head was buried in his hands and whose shoulders shook with uncontrolled paroxysms of sorrow. Her motherly instinct prompted her to console the man, but she restrained herself with the thought that he was a stranger and might resent her interference. All that day and the day after she spent her waking hours surreptitiously watching him sniffle into his handkerchief. On the third morning, while the train was already winding its way through the orange groves of California, she could stand it no longer. "My poor boy," she said as she patted him on the shoulder. "Maybe if you tell me what is breaking your heart, it will make you feel better."

The young man looked up at her and wrung his hands. "For three days now," he sobbed, "I've been on the wrong train."

»»✳««

A RESOURCEFUL MISSIONARY fell into the hands of a band of cannibals. "Going to eat me, I take it," said the missionary. "You wouldn't like me." He took out his pocket-knife, sliced a piece from the calf of his leg, and handed it to the chief. "Try it, and see for yourself," he urged. The chief took one bite, grunted, and spat.

The missionary remained on the island fifty years. He had a cork leg.

(168)

JIM CROWDER, famous Midwest book magnate, got a seat on a crowded railroad diner one day. "Do you like split pea soup?" asked the waiter.

"No," said Jim.

"Chicken croquettes?"

"No."

The waiter took the napkin off the table. "Good day," he said. "You is had your lunch."

»»✳««

WITH A DIME clutched tightly in her hand, a little ten-year-old girl seated herself at a soda counter in a Mid-Western drugstore and said, "I want a sundae with one scoop of cherry ice-cream and one scoop of banana. Put a dash of marshmallow on it and some chopped nuts, a little maple syrup and four cherries on top."

The man behind the counter gravely replied, "Your order will be obeyed, Your Majesty, but would you mind coming back next Wednesday morning for a fitting?"

»»✳««

REGULARLY each year for ten years Mrs. Grover Cleveland Filliken presented her husband with a bouncing new baby, and there followed the business of going to the local church for the christening. The first baby was named Eustace William Jennings Bryan Euripides Obadiah Filliken. Each succeeding baby had a name that was a little bit longer and more elaborate. When she arrived with the eleventh baby, the vicar was waiting for her with a stern look on his face. "Mrs. Filliken," he said, "I am sorry to say that our little parish has reached the end of its resources. From now on you really must bring your own ink."

ENGLISH SOCIETY was agog when a great Duke married a little blonde from the Music Hall chorus. It was even more agog when a Bond Street art gallery put on exhibition a lifesized portrait of her in the altogether. The Duke was furious. "I don't know what's biting you," said his wife. "Believe me, honeybun, there's nothing wrong. *He did it from memory*."

»»*««

LITTLE MICHAEL was spending his first night under his Aunt Minnie's roof. She came in to hear him say his prayers. "You did beautifully, Michael," she told him, when he had finished.

"That was nothing," boasted Michael. "You oughta hear me gargle."

»»*««

A SCOTSMAN who had worked for many years on railroads in his native land, came to the U. S. and settled in a remote section of the Middle West. Soon after his arrival there was a project for a railroad through the district.

"Hoot, mon," said the Scot to a neighbor who brought the tidings, "ye canna build a railroad across this country."

"And why not, Ferguson?"

"Why not? You ask me, 'Why not'? Dinna ye see the country's flat as a floor? Ye hae nae place at all t' run your toonels thru."

»»*««

TWO PENNILESS lads arrived here from Europe. The first one made a million dollars. He invented a machine into which you inserted a dime and a new wife came out. The other made ten million. In his machine you inserted the wife and a new dime came out.

(170)

MR. BECKER'S FACE lit up as he recognized the man who was walking ahead of him down the subway stairs. He clapped the man so heartily on the back that the man nearly collapsed, and cried, "Goldberg, I hardly recognized you. Why, you've gained thirty pounds since I saw you last, and you've had your nose fixed, and I swear you are about two feet taller." The man looked at him angrily. "I beg your pardon," he said in icy tones, "but I do not happen to be Goldberg."

"Aha," said Mr. Becker. "You've even changed your name."

»»*««

A LEARNED RABBI of Minsk wanted to take a trip to Pinsk. He went over to Schmul's stable and arranged for Schmul to drive him over in a horse and buggy. The trip proceeded without incident until they came to the first real hill. Halfway up the horse stopped dead and wouldn't move another step until Schmul got out and walked alongside the buggy to the top of the hill. At the next hill both Schmul and the rabbi had to get out in order to reach the summit. Then came the biggest hill of all. First Schmul got out. Then the rabbi got out. Finally the exasperated men had to unharness the nag and pull the buggy to the top themselves.

By that time the gleaming towers of Pinsk were visible in the distance. The remaining miles were covered in due course and the rabbi prepared to part company with Schmul.

"Schmul," he said, "that I had to go from Minsk to Pinsk, that was my business. That you had to go—well, I paid you to come with me. But tell me, Schmul: why did you bring the horse?"

VINCENT STARRETT tells a story of a Turkish Sultan who awoke his current favorite in a great state of excitement. "Quick," he cried, "give me my spectacles before I wake up." When the favorite brought them to him, he explained, "I'm having a beautiful dream, but there are one or two things in it I can't clearly make out."

»»✳««

A MEDICAL STUDENT found the first question in an examination: "Name five reasons why mother's milk is better for babies than cow's milk." He answered, "First, because it is fresher; second, it is cleaner; third, the cats can't get it; fourth, it is easier to take to movies and to picnics. Then he thought for a moment and added, "Fifth, it comes in such a cute little container."

He passed.

»»✳««

IRWIN EDMAN tells about the little shaver who was crying his eyes out on the sidestreet curbstone. Both of his parents, he informed the good samaritan who stopped to console him, were dead, and his only living relative, a brother, was up in Harvard. "Well," said the samaritan, "a brother at Harvard! That's mighty fine. What is he studying there?"

"Oh, he ain't studying anything," sobbed the boy. "*They're* studying *him*."

»»✳««

A MILLIONAIRE soap manufacturer graciously consented to a press interview. "To what do you attribute your success?" asked one reporter.

"To clean living my friend, to clean living," said the soap man earnestly.

(172)

OF DUBIOUS authenticity is the story about John D. Rocke-feller, Sr., registering at the Willard Hotel in Washington and asking for the cheapest room without bath. The hotel clerk was dumbfounded. "But, Mr. Rockefeller," he pro-tested. "When your son stops here he always occupies the finest suite we have."

"My son has a rich father," said Mr. Rockefeller sternly. "I am not so fortunate."

»»*««

THE OWNER of a corner saloon was sleeping peacefully at 3 o'clock in the morning when his phone rang: "What time does your saloon open?" asked a drunken voice.

"Eleven o'clock," said the saloon-keeper, and slammed down the phone.

A minute later the bell rang again. The same voice asked "What time did you say your saloon opened?"

"Eleven o'clock, damn it," roared the proprietor, "and you can't get in a minute before."

"Who wants to get in?" said a very hurt voice. "I want to get out."

»»*««

DURING ONE of the tensest moments of a murder picture at the Paramount Theatre in New York, an elderly gentleman began groping for something on the floor, greatly disturbing a lady in the next seat. "What have you lost?" she inquired testily.

"A caramel," said the man.

"You're going to all this bother for a measly caramel?" she asked.

"Yes," was the reply. "My teeth are in it."

(173)

A MAN who discovered the joys of fishing rather late in life became even more insistent than ordinary anglers upon recounting his triumphs to skeptical acquaintances. Enraged by their thinly veiled hints that he was a liar, he bought a pair of scales, installed them in his library, and made his friends watch while he actually weighed the fish he had caught. One evening, a neighbor burst in and excitedly sought permission to borrow the scale. He was back in ten minutes, his face flushed with delight. "Congratulate me," he cried. "I am the father of a forty-eight pound baby boy."

»»✳««

A MANUFACTURER received a whopping bill from his lawyer. He stood for everything until he came to this item: "For crossing street to talk to you and discovering it wasn't you: $500."

»»✳««

A SALESMAN in San Francisco wired his home office in New York, "Dear Boss: This is a matter of life and death. I am broke, starving, and they locked me out of my room. For God's sake, wire me $50 or I am a dead duck."

He handed the blank to the telegraph operator and said, "Please don't read this back to me. I couldn't stand it."

»»✳««

THE CHILDREN'S PARTY was drawing to a close and the cook triumphantly brought in the *pièce de résistance*—a heaping platter of jello. As she put it on the table, it quivered and shook. Most of the children exclaimed with delight, but one started to leave the table. "None of that for me," he said firmly. "It's not dead yet."

(174)

THE COUNTRY'S most high-powered insurance salesman found his six-year-old son out on the lawn when he came home, clutching a ball and bat. "Watch me, Daddy," commanded the son. "I will hit it out of sight." He tossed the ball up and took a roundhouse swing and missed. "Strike one," he called with no diminishing of his enthusiasm. "Watch me connect with this one." He missed again. "Strrrrike two," he chanted. "Well, Daddy, you always tell me it only takes one to hit it. This is it." A third time he took a swipe at the ball and a third time went down swinging. "Three strikes and out," he announced. "Oh, boy, am I a pitcher!"

»»*««

THREE STOUT LADIES were slowly rocking their chairs on the porch of a summer hotel on a hot summer afternoon. The first lady had twenty diamond bracelets on her arm, the second an even dozen, and the third just one.

"When my bracelets get dirty," said No. One loftily, "I drive in my Rolls straight to Tiffany's. My footman takes them in for me. Mr. Tiffany himself takes two days off to polish them."

"My bracelets give me trouble, too," confessed No. Two. "When they need cleaning, I take my Buick to Lambert's. I give them to the manager. For six hours he cleans them."

The two ladies turned expectantly to No. Three. "And you?" asked One, with a slight smirk, "What do you do, Mrs. Gaines?"

Mrs. Gaines was unperturbed. "I never bother cleaning *my* diamond bracelets," she announced calmly. "When I see they've gotten dirty—I just throw them away."

(175)

THE LITTLE Scotch couple shared a seat on the train from Edinburgh to London. At every way station the man would hop out of the train and buy two tickets for the next station. The conductor finally got tired of punching the fares. "Where are you two bound or?" he inquired grimly.

"London," said the Scotsman.

"Then why the devil don't you buy two through tickets and save me all this bother?" asked the conductor.

"Ah," said the Scotsman, "the doctor tells me my wife has a very weak heart and it is likely to give out any minute."

»» ✳ ««

MR. PERKINS was painfully limping down the street when he met a friend, who expressed great concern over his condition. After a few questions, the friend told him, "I had the same trouble a few months ago, but I had all my teeth removed, and now I'm fit as a fiddle. I strongly suggest that you do the same thing."

Feeling that he had nothing to lose, Mr. Perkins had all *his* teeth removed, but in vain. Several weeks later, still limping, he ran into another friend who told him that he cured a similar condition by having his appendix removed. So Mr. Perkins had his appendix removed, but still he limped. A third friend suggested removing his tonsils, but that too failed.

Some months after his first encounter, Mr. Perkins, a cured man, was strutting gaily along when he ran into friend number one. "Ah, I see you're all right now," said his pal. "So my advice worked."

"No, taking my teeth out didn't help; taking out my appendix and my tonsils didn't help. But I'll tell you what did help. I took the nail out of my shoe."

(176)

McDUFF AWOKE one morning and found that his wife beside him had died in her sleep. Sadly he called down to the pantry. "Only one boiled egg for breakfast this morning, Dorrit."

»»✳««

A MIAMI NEWSPAPER relates the touching story of a married couple who had not spoken to each other since 1935, but were reconciled during a recent hurricane. They were blown simultaneously through the roof of their home, and the wife explained later, "It seemed silly for us to go out together and not be speaking."

»»✳««

AN AMERICAN SOLDIER, billeted in England, didn't like the way the food was cooked at a local inn. He barely touched the food that was set down before him. The waiter was indignant. "Aren't you ashamed to be wasting food that way?" he chided. "Don't you know that food will win the war?"

"Could be," allowed the American, "but who's going to get the enemy to eat here?"

»»✳««

A PERSONAL AD in a Los Angeles paper: Young girl with two cans of corn would like to meet gentleman with can of lima beans. Object: succotash.

»»✳««

A PARSON was introduced to a Mrs. Hummock and tried to fix her name in his mind by rhyming it with stummock. The next day he met her and yoohooed, "How do you do, Mrs. Kelly?"

»»✳««

MR. CARTMELL described his morning round as Civil War golf. "Went out in 61," he explained, "and came back in 65."

DALE WARREN, the Boston Casanova, was reminiscing to a friend. "I know nine girls on Pickney Street alone," he informed him.

"All told?" asked the friend.

"No," said Warren. "One of them kept her trap shut."

»»✳««

A MAN bought a watch and chain from a Jersey City dealer. The proprietor handed him a revolver with the package.

"What's this for?" asked the man.

"You bought a gold watch," was the explanation. "You want to *keep* it, don't you?"

»»✳««

RING LARDNER liked to tell his friends of an eccentric in the Adirondacks who constructed a building entirely of knot holes. "What kind of holes do you call these?" asked a visiting New Yorker.

"They are knot holes," said the builder.

"Hmmpf," said the New Yorker, "they look like holes to me."

»»✳««

A FEW of Mark Twain's oft-quoted remarks: "Water, if taken in moderation, cannot hurt anybody"; "Fear knocked at the door. Faith answered. No one was there"; "When some men discharge an obligation, you can hear the report for miles around"; "Everybody is always talking about the weather, but nobody ever does anything about it"; "When I was a boy of fourteen, my father was so ignorant I could hardly stand to have the old man around. But when I got to

(178)

be twenty-one, I was astonished at how much the old man had learned in seven years."

»»*««

DR. OTIS MOORE watched a very little girl pull a very big weed from her Victory garden. "You must be pretty strong to pull out such a big weed," he remarked.

"Yes," agreed the youngster. "Don't forget that the whole world was pulling on the other side."

»»*««

A MAN received a big check for services rendered, but discovered that it was one cent short. A stickler for detail, he insisted that the discrepancy be repaired and, in due course, received another check for a single penny. He presented it for payment at his bank. The teller examined it closely and asked him, "How would you like this, sir? Heads or tails?"

»»*««

TWO FRIENDS motored home from a fishing trip in Maine. On a lonely country road they encountered engine trouble. Who answered their knock at the nearest farmhouse? Right! The farmer's beautiful daughter. She gave them dinner and let them stay overnight. Six months later one of the friends received an ominous-looking legal document. A frown disappeared as he read it, and then he phoned his fishing companion.

"I say, Tom," he said. "Did you by any chance spend a little time with that beautiful farm girl the night our car broke down?"

"Why, yes," answered Tom sheepishly.

"And did you, in a moment of Machiavellian cunning, give her my name and address?"

(179)

"Now, don't get sore about that," broke in Tom. "Where's your sense of humor?"

"Oh, I'm not a bit sore," his friend assured him. "I just thought you'd like to know I heard from her lawyer. She died last week and left me the farm and $12,000 in cash."

A Handful of Laughing Stock Definitions (Webster's? Noah! Noah!)

ADAM: The only wolf who couldn't use the opening gambit, "Excuse me, but haven't I seen you somewhere before?"

Adherent: A follower who has not yet gotten all he expects. (Ambrose Bierce)

Adult: A person who has stopped growing at both ends and is now growing in the middle.

After-dinner speaker: The art of diluting a two-minute idea with a two-hour vocabulary.

Alimony: The high cost of leaving.

Amazon: First part of a sentence. Example: Well, amazon of a gun.

Automaton: A gent who eats at the automat.

Baby: An alimentary canal with a loud voice at one end and no responsibility at the other. (E. Adamson)

Banker: A man who lends you an umbrella when the sun is shining and wants it back the minute it starts to rain.

Banquet: A plate of cold, hairy chicken and artificially colored green peas completely surrounded by dreary speeches and appeals for donations.

Brassier: An invention designed to make a mountain out of a molehill, and vice versa.

Bubble bath: There's no place like foam.

Buccaneer: What you'll pay for corn if inflation sets in.

Canoe: Floating conveyance which should be treated like a mischievous boy: it behaves better when paddled from the rear.

Centaur: A man with a horse where his pants ought to be.

Consideration: A woman who shoots her husband with a bow and arrow because she doesn't want to wake the children.

Consult: To seek another's advice on a course already decided upon. (Bierce)

Consultant: A man who knows less about your business than you do and gets paid more for telling you how to run it than you could possibly make out of it even if you ran it right instead of the way he told you.

Co-signer: A damn fool with a fountain pen.

Counterfeit money: Pseudough.

Crook: A business rival who has just left the room.

Cynic: A man who knows the price of everything and the value of nothing. (Oscar Wilde)

Diamond: Rich man's rhinestone.

Epigram: A wise-crack that has played Carnegie Hall. (Oscar Levant)

Experience: Business man's definition of his own mistake.

Expert: An ordinary citizen, away from home, giving advice.

Fishing: An uninhabited body of water completely surrounded by liars in old clothes.

Forger: A man who makes a name for himself.

Genealogist: One who traces back your family as far as your money will go.

Gentleman: A man who never, unintentionally, gives offense. (Wm. Feather)

Good manners: The noise you don't make when you're eating soup.

Gossamer: The nearest thing to nothing—and better in black.

History: A record of events which never should have happened. ("Time")

Incongruous: That's where the laws are made.

Kiss: An operation, cunningly devised, for the mutual stoppage of speech at a moment when words are utterly superfluous. (Oliver Herford)

Love: One darn thing after another.

Male quartette: An animal that has eight legs and flies.

Marriage: Public confession of a strictly private intention. (Ian Hay)

Meteorologist: A man who can look into a girl's eyes and tell whether.

Mink: When a woman turns around to look at another woman—that's mink!

Monologue: One woman talking. (Not to be confused with Catalogue: two women talking.)

Negligee: What she hopes she'll have on when the house burns down.

Oboe: An ill wood-wind that nobody blows good.

Optimist: A husband who comes home, finds the place littered with tired cigar butts, and exclaims, "Thank heavens, my wife has given up cigarettes at last."

Oratory: The art of making a loud noise seem like a deep thought.

Parrot: Only living creature with power of speech con-

(186)

tent to repeat just what it hears without trying to make a good story of it.

Undignified: The action of a competitor that the man who uses the word wishes he could do himself.

Wolf: A man who takes out a sweater girl and tries to pull the wool over her eyes. Tired same: One who hopes the girl will say no.

Limerick Lane

WHEN IT COMES to that form of facetious jingle called "limericks," the editor of this compendium votes with the "I-can-take-'em-or-leave-'em" contingent. Limericks made their first appearance in England about 1820, were popularized a quarter of a century later by Edward Lear, and have flourished since, for the most part in college comic magazines, advertising contests and salesmen's conventions. Choicest specimens of the latter variety are omitted from this volume as a token of respect to the publishers and the United States Post Office.

> A bookworm from Kennebunk, Me.
> Found pleasure in reading Monte.,
> But he got little wallop
> From Miss Winsor's trollop,
> And "Finnegan's Wake" caused him pe.

A Chinaman down in Ky.
Complained to a friend, "Me unly.
The Southern chop suey
Is how you say? Phooey?
And when they bring check, I am sty."

A farmer once called his cow "Zephyr";
She seemed such an amiable hephyr.
When the farmer drew near,
She kicked off his ear,
Which made him considerably dephyr.

There was a young lady named Shanker
Who dozed while a ship lay at anchor.
She woke in dismay
When she heard the mate say,
"Let's hoist up the topsheet and spanker."

There was a young lady named Bright
Whose speed was much faster than light.
She went out one day
In a relative way
And returned on the previous night.

There was an old man from Calcutta
Who had a most terrible stutter.
"G-g-give me," he said,
Some b-b-b-read,
And b-b-b-b-b-b-butter."

Said an ape as he swung by his tail
To his children, both female and male.
"From your offspring, my dears,
In a couple of years,
May evolve a professor at Yale!"

There was a young girl from Pawtucket
Who went down to Hell in a bucket.
And when she got there
And they asked for her fare
She said, "I propose that we ducat."

There was a young man from the city
Who met what he thought was a kitty.
He gave it a pat
And said, "Nice little cat."
They buried his clothes, out of pity.

There was a young lady named Maude
A sort of society fraud.
In the parlor, 'tis told
She was distant and cold
But on the veranda, my Gawd!

A senora who strolled on the Corso
Displayed quite a lot of her torso.
A crowd soon collected
And no one objected
Though some were in favor of more so.

A wonderful bird is the pelican
His mouth can hold more than his belican.
He can take in his beak
Enough food for a week.
I'm darned if I know how the helican.

There was a young teacher in Fla.
Whose behavior grew torrid and Ta.
Till an impetuous student
Became quite impudent
And kissed her right out in the Ca.

There was a young man from Madras
Whose nostrils were made out of glass.
When he twitched them together
They played "Stormy Weather,"
Which startled King Hailie-Selasse.

A painter who came from Great Britain
Hailed a lady who sat with her knitain.
He remarked with a sigh,
"That park bench—well, I
Just painted it, right where you're sitain."

I once took the bishop to tea
It was just as I thought it would be
His rumblings abdominal
Were simply phenomenal
And everyone thought it was me.

The ersatz they served in Berlin
Made a once-buxom lady so thin
That when she essayed
To drink lemonade
She slipped through the straw and fell in.

In a notable family called Stein
There's Gertrude, there's Ep, and there's Ein.
Gert's writing is hazy
Ep's statues are crazy,
And nobody understands Ein.

The bottle of perfume that Willie sent
Was highly offensive to Millicent.
Her thanks were so cold
That they quarreled, I'm told,
Through that silly scent Willie sent Millicent.

A damsel at Vassar named Breeze,
Weighed down with B. Lits and D.D.'s,
Collapsed from the strain.
Said her doctor, "It's plain
You are killing yourself—by degrees."

The fact is that Rome needed money
And, further, the Gauls got too funny.
So they sent out some legions
To clean up them regions.
J. Caesar? Yep, he was there, sonny.

A senator Rex Asinorum
Was needed to make up a quorum.
So he flew down from Venice
Asked "Who knows where my pen is?"
Then laconically scribbled "I'm forum."

A lady from Atlanta, Ga.
Became quite a notable fa.
But she faded from view
With a quaint I.O.U.
That she signed "Mrs. Lucrezia Ba."

A striptease named Cubbard in Kansas
Made a fortune by wiggling her Frances.
When the censors got there
Miss Cubbard was bare
She explained, "I don't know where my fans is."

A student who lives up in Worcester
Is reading much more than he ucester.
He's filled up his closet
with reprints from Grosset
And acrostics from Simon and Schucester.

Last Laughs

THERE IS a chronic shortage of dependable servants in Hollywood, and Hedy Lamarr considered herself a lucky lady when she snared an impeccable English butler into her service. He had only one minor fault. He *would* insist on walking into her boudoir without knocking. Miss Lamarr finally lost her patience. "Grosvenor," she declared. "I am telling you for the last time that I will not have you enter my dressing room without knocking." "Control yourself, madam," said the imperturbable Grosvenor. "I always peek through the keyhole first, and if you have nothing on, I don't enter."

At least that's what an MGM press release declares he said. By a strange coincidence a butler of Anna Held's said the same thing when the story went round about 1904. Could it be the same sly Grosvenor, up to his old tricks? Or—perish the thought—the same press agent?

HAROLD E. STASSEN, sometime Governor of Minnesota, naval hero, and possible presidential candidate in the next election, tells about a Swede in Duluth who invited an acquaintance to his wedding anniversary. "My house bane tird on right on Criley Alley," he explained. "Push bell with elbow and when door open, put foot against it and push way in." "Why will I have to use my elbow and foot?" the acquaintance asked. "By jiminy," said the Swede in a menacing tone. "You not coming empty-handed, I hope!"

»»✻««

"I'D LIKE you to come right over," a man phoned an undertaker, "and supervise the burial of my poor, departed wife."

"Your wife!" gasped the undertaker. "Didn't I bury her two years ago?"

"You don't understand," said the man. "You see, I married again."

"Oh," said the undertaker. "Congratulations!"

»»✻««

THE TAXICAB stopped in front of Dolores del Fromage's patio with a jerk, who got out. Dolores was his passion flower. She had climbed the ladder, wrong by wrong, and had just enough brains to sit down when she was tired. Fortunately, girls built like Dolores didn't need brains. She had a wonderful profile all the way down. The jerk frequently declared that only two good things had come out of Hollywood that year, and that Dolores had both of them.

The jerk was not exactly a spring chicken. His friends swore that he had known Madame Butterfly when she was a caterpillar.

(202)

"Leave us be going to the Stork Club," whistled the jerk through his store teeth. "They won't let you in there," Dolores reminded him. "Don't you remember they threw you out on your ear last night?"

"Tonight," vowed the jerk, "will be different. I'm going in there and throw every one of them bums out. I want you should stand on the sidewalk and count them as they hit the asphalt."

Dolores could count straight through to seven so she agreed to take a chance. The jerk strode boldly into the entrance of the Stork. A moment later a body hurtled out and landed in a grotesque heap in the spot where taxicabs stood in the days when there were still taxis.

"One," chortled Dolores gaily. "No, no," came the jerk's voice from the gutter. "Don't start counting yet. It's me again."

»»*««

A MUSICIAN married a painfully ugly woman for her money and dragged her with him to one soiree after another. A friend said, "I can understand your marrying her to get your hands on all that dough, but why do you have to bring her with you every time you go out?" The musician explained, "It's easier than kissing her goodbye."

»»*««

A PUBLISHER once got a staggering bill for a consultation with the late legal light, Max Steuer. The next day the publisher bumped into Steuer in the elevator. "Mr. Steuer," he said, "it's nice to see you again. Remember, Mr. Steuer, I am not asking your opinion about this. I'm telling you."

(203)

Bob Considine tells a story about a broken down prize-fighter who appeared in one of the preliminaries of a fourth-rate club one Christmas Eve. It was a miserable night, with a near blizzard sweeping the city and holding the attendance down to a mere handful. The fighter took a terrible beating. His nose was broken, his shoulder dislocated and one eye badly bruised by the final blow that spelled finis to the match. When he came to in his dressing room, his manager told him sadly that his share of the purse was only $10.00. $5.00 of this, of course, went to the manager and another $2.00 to his seconds. A charitable doctor agreed to patch him up for $2.00 more. That left him with exactly $1.00 to show for his night's agonizing work. As he staggered to the door, he found eight faithful fans awaiting his appearance. He herded them all into the lunch wagon across the way and ordered nine hamburgers. "That'll be 90¢" said the chef behind the counter. The old pug fished out his last dollar and flipped it onto the counter with a magnificent gesture. Church bells were just beginning to peal as he reached the door of the diner. He tightened his flimsy coat about the neck and, with a wave of his hand to the waiter, called, "Keep the change. *Easy come, easy go.*"

»»✲««

One of the professors at a London medical college was appointed honorary physician to the king, and proudly wrote a notice on his classroom blackboard informing his students of this great event in his life.

When he returned to his classroom that afternoon the students jumped to their feet and solemnly sang "God Save the King."

(204)

Bob Hope and Bing Crosby are inseparable golfing companions, but Hope has no great regard for the calibre of Crosby's game—on paper, anyhow. "Universal Pictures," he asserts, "used one of Bing's divots for the flying carpet in 'Ali Baba and the Forty Thieves.' Another time der Bingle sent the follow-through of a mashie shot flying over the Lockheed plant. The foreman pointed to it and yelled to his men, 'Get busy, boys. Look what they're turning out over at Douglas.' "

»»*««

Medical circles in San Mateo were astounded recently when a man bit himself squarely on his posterior. He sat on his false teeth.

»»*««

"Eustace," called Mama, "Are you spitting into that fish bowl?"

"No, Ma, but I'm coming mighty close."

»»*««

A man driving North on Central Avenue found himself behind a coupé whose driver extended an arm to indicate a left turn. He swerved to the right, but at that moment an arm shot out of the coupé indicating a right turn. When this process had been repeated twice more, the irritated driver drove up to the coupé to deliver a few pointed remarks. He found it occupied by two angry women. "And *I* say," the one on the right was shrilling, "dot Yonkers is *dis* way."

»»*««

A drunken gent sashayed into a barber shop and demanded a haircut. "You'll have to remove your hat first," said the barber. "Shorry, old man," said the drunk. "I didn't know there wash ladies preshent."

(205)

HARRY EMERSON FOSDICK quotes an essay that a young schoolgirl once wrote on the subject of Queen Victoria. "When Queen Victoria was coronated, she took as her motto 'I will be good.' She followed this motto passionately throughout a long and tedious life."

»»✳««

OLD MOSE received an anonymous letter one day which contained a single sentence: "If you don't stop stealing my chickens, I'm gonna cut out your gizzard." Mose was so bothered that he consulted the local constable, who laughed, and said, "Well, all you've got to do is stop stealing the chickens." "You don' seem to understand," said Mose. "Dis letter am *unanimous*. Whose chickens is I supposed to stop stealin'?"

»»✳««

ONE OF THE late Irvin Cobb's favorite stories concerned a Tammany ward heeler who enlisted the aid of a corps of repeaters to clinch a particularly close assembly election. The leader of the motley crew was a freckled, red-headed specimen with County Clare written all over his map. When the election clerk asked his name, however, he looked hard at a slip of paper in his hand and said, "Isadore Shapiro."

"What nonsense," sneered a challenger from the opposition forces. "That's not your name and you know it."

"It is too," said the repeater, "and what's more, I'm gonna vote under it, despite what any hatchet-faced shrimp like you may have to say about it."

The ward heeler heard the argument and slapped his man heartily on the back. "That's me boy, Clancy. Don't let nobody bluff you. Soitn'ly your name is Shapiro!"

(206)

THE BETTER Business Bureau spotted a beach concessionaire who are selling adulterated syrups. "What's a wrong with that?" he demanded. "Customers like, and no getta sick." "There's a pure food law in this state," an official explained patiently. "You've got to tell the truth about the ingredients of the products you sell." The concessionaire reluctantly promised to put up a sign, but reported in delight a month later that it had doubled his business. The official looked at the sign. In big red letters it proclaimed "Every drink sold here is guaranteed to be highly adulterated."

»»✳««

A COLORED KID, reports Quote, asked his mother for a quarter to take to school. "What fo'?" asked the mother. "Teacher say hit t'help po' folks," said the son. "Humph!" commented the mother. "What you think we is if we ain't po' folks? You go tell that teacher Ah say taken you offen de givin' list and put you on de *gittin'* list!"

»»✳««

COMMANDER WALTER DAY reminds me of the old Scotchman (Sandy, of course) who used to come home drunk every night, greatly to his wife's annoyance. Thinking to cure him once and for all, she put a sheet around her shoulders and hid behind a hedge one dark night. In due course, Sandy came weaving down the lane and, when he was nearly abreast of her, she jumped out before him. "Sandy," she said in sepulchral tones, "do ye ken who I am?" "Noo," replied the dazed Sandy. "Well," said his wife, "I am the ould Nick and I coom to carry ye awa'." "Aweel, aweel," said Sandy. "Gie us your hand, laddie. I am married to your sister."

(207)

A WASHINGTON society leader hosted a big luncheon to help launch a new Red Cross drive. One of the high dignitaries in attendance patted the hostess' little daughter on the head and said, "Aren't we a big help to our dear mother. What is our task for today?" "Our task for today," snapped the little daughter, "is to see that none of you bozos try to get away with any of the silver."

»»✳««

IN THE COURSE of Queen Victoria's Diamond Jubilee, the diminutive Princess Liluiokalani of the Sandwich Islands (now Hawaii) curtsied to Victoria and said, "I too have English blood in my veins, Your Majesty." Victoria said "How come?" or words to that effect. "You see," beamed the Princess, "My ancestors ate Captain Cook."

»»✳««

JUDGE PECORA recalls a vacation he spent in a Maine fishing village. "Got a criminal lawyer in these parts?" he asked the keeper of the general store. "We think we have," was the answer, "but we can't prove it on him."

»»✳««

GEORGE JEAN NATHAN's angry review of John Barrymore's clowning performance in "My Dear Children" began, "I always said that I'd like Barrymore's acting till the cows came home. Well, ladies and gentlemen, last night the cows came home." Another eminent critic, Wolcott Gibbs, wound up a paragraph on one of the worst "turkeys" that ever hit Broadway with the comment, "This is a fine sample of what happens when somebody just goes out of his way to write a play."

(208)

"499 Scottish Stories for the Price of 500" is the eye-catching title of a new collection whipped up by B. C. Forbes, well-known business analyst. They kilt me. Choice specimen: An Aberdonian walked into a high-class restaurant, dined well, and, paying his check, pushed a penny toward the efficient waitress. She looked at the picayune tip, registered dissatisfaction. "Even the champion miser of Aberdeen tips us tuppence when he eats here," she declared. The unabashed Aberdonian waved his hand and announced dramatically, "Gaze on the new champion."

Mr. Forbes also is authority for the report that two taxis collided in Princes Street, Edinburgh, in the wee small hours after a dance. Eleven of the passengers were detained at the infirmary, but the other seven went home after treatment.

Forbes asked one of his countrymen, "How d'ye like your new radio?" "It is fine, man," was the answer, "but it's awfa' hard tae read by the wee licht."

»»*««

THE CHICAGO TRIBUNE carried a story about a Yank soldier in the Philippine jungle who picked some luscious looking berries, but was afraid they might be poisonous. A native lad watched him without comment. The Yank pointed first to the berries, then to his mouth, then went through the motions of eating, but the boy remained impassive while the performance was repeated several times. Finally another G.I. came along. "I've been trying to find out," said the first one, "whether or not it was safe to eat these berries." The Filipino boy's face lit up. "Hell, yes," he said, "They got Vitamin B. Whyn't 'cha ask me?"

(209)

Two FLASHILY DRESSED individuals, obviously big market operators, were discussing their deals in voices loud enough to be heard from one end of the day coach to the other. "When I first looked into that stock it was selling at 23," lamented one. "I've watched it go up steadily to 40, to 50, and then to 60, and dammit, I never bought a share." "Think it's good for a still further rise?" asked the other. "I certainly do," asserted the first. "You mark my words. Before it's finished, that stock'll sell at a dollar."

»»*««

DURING THE taxicab shortage in New York, a popular refrain was

> "It isn't raining rain, you know.
> It's hailing taxicabs."

One bejeweled and beminked dowager, opera bound, despaired of getting a cab, and condescended to travel by BMT. As she swayed on a strap she remarked loudly to her escort, "This is the first time I've been on this smelly subway in twenty years." An old man seated nearby informed her gravely, "Lady, we've missed you!"

»»*««

A GREEK PROFESSOR tore his suit and took it to a tailor who actually had been born in Athens. The tailor examined the suit and asked, "Euripides?" "Yes," said the professor. "Eumenides."

»»*««

DESCRIPTION of a cow followed by a couple of ducks: milk and quackers.

A FRAIL, tired little man told his doctor that the demands of his 200-pound wife were just about killing him. "I work twelve hours a day to support her in a style to which she never was accustomed," he said bitterly, "and then I have to stay up until three or four every morning doing the rhumba and the conga with her in night clubs."

"No woman can stand a nightly routine of that sort," the doc assured him. "Let her have her way absolutely for one year—give in to her every whim—and you have my assurance that a year from today she'll be dead."

"You give me hope," said the man. "Can I count on it?"

"You have my guarantee," said the doctor.

The scene now shifts to the little man's back yard exactly 364 days later. By this time he was such a wreck that he had to be wheeled around in a chair, and his hands shook so that he had to use both of them to get a glass of orange juice to his lips. He sat bundled up in two rugs, shivering, and watching his wife, huskier than ever, beating a rug. Every time she followed through with her beater, the clothes-line quivered like a violin string, and the rug flew into the breeze. She packed all the wallop of a giant tank.

The little man watched her in wonder, and cackled to himself. "And to think that this time tomorrow she'll be dead."

»»✳««

THE LAST TIME Eddie Cantor came East from Hollywood, he declared that his train left from Tracks Seven, Eight, and Nine. "Must have been a mighty long train," commented somebody. "It wasn't that," said Cantor. "It was the new lady engineer. She brought the train in sideways."

(2 1 1)

Two UPSTATE CITIZENS were boasting of the respective renown of their local rabbis.

"Everybody knows Rabbi Cohen of Syracuse," said one. "When he goes to Washington, he is invited to stay at the White House."

"What's that?" deprecated the other. "A few years before the war our Rabbi Solomon of Buffalo visited Rome, and took a walk with the Pope. You know what happened? Hundreds of Italians asked, 'Who's that bald-headed little fellow with Rabbi Solomon?' "

»»✻««

A PUBLISHER was dandling his pretty secretary on his lap one afternoon when the wife barged in unexpectedly. The publisher, with magnificent presence of mind, said, "And take this wire, Miss Kreiswirth: Atlas Furniture Company. Gents: I don't want to hear any more about critical shortages. I simply cannot continue to maintain my office efficiently with only one chair."

»»✻««

MR. AND MRS. TOPLITZ were having their first dinner at a fancy restaurant, and were considerably puzzled when the waitress put finger bowls in front of them at the conclusion of their repast. "It can't be coffee, because we've already had coffee, and besides it doesn't look like coffee," reasoned Mr. Toplitz. "I think I'll ask the waitress." "No, papa," begged his wife. "Don't let her think we're yokels." But Mr. Toplitz was not to be dissuaded. "or what are these things?" he inquired. "They're finger bowls," said the waitress with a superior smile. "You see," exulted Mrs. Toplitz. "You ask a foolish question; you get a foolish answer!"

HENRY MORTON ROBINSON is a punster to be reckoned with in any man's league. His wife came running to him one day as he was digging potatoes in his garden. "Doctor Perkins," she reported, "has become a naval surgeon." "Ah," said Henry. "What a specialist." "You aren't as gallant as you were when a boy," pouted his wife. "No," said Henry, "and you aren't as buoyant as you were when a gal." At this moment his Pomeranian barked at him (the dog was a bit of a critic). Henry booted the pup and remarked blithely, "I have no intention of letting a Pom de terre me." He then burst into his theme song: "Orange Juice Sorry That I Made You Cry?"

»»✳««

A WAITERS' MANUAL suggests that any one of the following five come-backs are appropriate when a customer complains "There's a fly in my soup":

1. Ssh! Everybody will want one!
2. What do you expect for a dime, elephants?
3. Wait'll you see the coffee!
4. That's all right. How much can a fly drink?
5. Force of habit, sir. Our chef used to be a tailor.

»»✳««

"PAW," said Mrs. Stimson over her knitting one night. "It's time you spoke a piece to our son Wilbur. 'Pears to me he jest plain don't want ter get hisself married."

"Don't you worry 'bout our Wilbur," soothed Mr. Stimson. "He'll marry fast enough when the wrong girl comes along."

(213)

THE WALL STREET Journal tells about an old French woman, extremely deaf, who lived across the street from a munitions plant being operated by the Nazis. One day an American shell made a direct hit, and the factory went up with a roar. The old lady heard the sound and said, "Come in, Yvette."

When the servant appeared, she added, "My hearing must be improving. That's the first time I've heard you knock on the door in twenty years."

»»✻««

ANOTHER STORY of the days when the American armies threw the Nazis out of France concerns a rabbit hunt that a grateful French landowner staged for some Yank officers. One of the Americans spotted a rabbit and was about to shoot when the Frenchman cried, "For God's sake, don't shoot. That is Robert. We never shoot at Robert." A few minutes later the party flushed another cottontail but again the Frenchman said, "No, no! That is Fru-Fru. It would not do to shoot at dear Fru-Fru." Finally a third rabbit bounded into sight. "Now," cried the Frenchman. "Fire at will, monsieurs. That is Francois. We *always* shoot at Francois!"

»»✻««

O'TOOLE REPORTED to the superintendent that a bit of an explosion had marred the day on a new construction job. "Anybody hurt in it?" queried the super. "Well, there was Clancy," recalled O'Toole. "He wint up with the divil of a bang." "How long did it take him to come down?" persisted the super. "Faith, an' I didn't see him come down," admitted O'Toole, "but if it didn't take him longer to get back than it took him to go up, he got back yistiday."

BACK FROM a winter vacation in sunny Florida, Joe E. Lewis reported that a high spot of his sojourn came when a beautiful young girl in the scantiest of bathing suits, came up and asked him to teach her how to swim. "I was doing magnificently with her," says Joe, "until some nosey life-guard came along and made us go in the water."

Lewis declares that Frankie Sinatra went in for a duck in the briny one morning. A fish looked him over and grumbled to a friend, "I've seen all kinds of bait in my time, but by Neptune, *this* is ridiculous!"

(215)

Lord Halifax amused a banquet audience gathered to honor him in Washington with the story of a tramp ship with a heterogeneous passenger list that stranded on an idyllic Polynesian islet.

Soon the little spot was a beehive of activity. The Germans were drilling the natives into an army. The Americans opened a general store and auto agency. The Australians started a race-track; the French a restaurant. Two Scots were financing the whole show, and a couple of Englishmen were still standing around waiting to be introduced.

»»✴««

A Pan-American Airlines pilot discovered that a colored mechanic had never been up in a plane, and took him up for a trial spin over Miami Bay one afternoon. When the plane came to a stop, the mechanic climbed out gingerly and said, "I shore is obliged for both ob dem rides." "Both?" queried the pilot. "There was only one." "Ah counts two," corrected the mechanic. "Mah fust'n and mah last'n."

»»✴««

Joe Laurie, Jr. knows a fellow who spent so much on his girl he finally had to marry her for his money.

»»✴««

"The time has arrived to take you to the operating room," said a doctor to his patient. "Now don't you worry about the outcome. I've lost my last eleven patients straight, and if there's anything at all in the law of averages, you should pull through. Is there anything I can do for you before we start?"

"There certainly is," said the patient grimly. "Help me on with my pants and vest."

"WAITER," commanded a big shot in a little restaurant, "bring us two orders of guiseppe verticelli." "Your pardon," said the waiter gently, "but that's the proprietor."

»»✳«««

A COLLEGE LAD had a ready excuse for his rebuff. "Her old man is a second-hand furniture dealer," he explained. "No wonder she wouldn't allow much on the old davenport."

»»✳«««

TWO MEN who had been fast friends in their boyhood but had not seen each other for years, met on 57th Street one afternoon. "You look great, Joe," chortled one. "What have you been doing with yourself?"

"I just got married," reported the other.

"That's good."

"Well, it's not so good. My wife is the ugliest dame in sixteen states."

"Oh, that's bad."

"Well, it's not so bad. She's worth about fourteen million dollars."

"Oh, that's good."

"Well, it's not so good. She's so stingy that she begrudges me a nickel for carfare every morning."

"Oh, that's bad."

"Well, it's not so bad. She owns a beautiful house on Fifth Avenue with forty-eight rooms."

"Oh, that's good."

"Well, it's not so good. The whole damn house burned to the ground last night."

"Oh, that's bad."

"Well, it's not so bad. My wife was in it."

KNUTE ROCKNE was once a guest-of-honor at a sports writers' dinner, and was seated at the elevated dais at the end of the banquet hall. The chairman had promised Rockne he wouldn't have to make a speech, but the general acclaim finally forced him to his feet. "Gentlemen," said Rockne, looking down at his well-fed and lubricated admirers. "You make me feel like the drunk in Central Park who looked into the lagoon, blinked with astonishment, and beckoned a cop to his side. 'Offisher,' he said, 'Isn't that the moon I shee in that water?' 'That it is,' said the cop. 'Heavens to Betsy,' marveled the drunk. 'How the devil did I ever get away up here?' "

»»*««

WHEN BURBAUM came up on a charge of burglary he insisted that he was competent to act as his own defence attorney. "There's no law against it," ruled the judge. "Go ahead."

Burbaum stamped up and down in front of the empty witness chair, and pointed a finger at it. "What's your name?" he inquired. Then he jumped into the chair and answered, "Jacob Burbaum."

Again he paced up and down the courtroom. "What's your business?" he asked. Bounding into the chair, he replied, "Cloaks and suits."

Now Burbaum really turned on the heat. Assuming a Napoleonic pose, he demanded, pausing between each word for dramatic effect. "And-where-were-you-on-the-night-of-January 18, 1945?"

Back in the witness box, the picture of innocence, he pointed to himself and said, "Who? Me?"

FAYE EMERSON not only became a picture star and married a president's son; she uncovered a brand new—well, *fairly* new kangaroo story. Pop Kangaroo turned to his wife and said, "Myrtle, where are Junior and the baby?" Myrtle looked down and cried with anguish, "Somebody has been picking my pocket."

»»*««

LOU HOLTZ tells about the kindly Mother Superior of a convent who took in a rather dim-witted refugee and made him official janitor of the establishment. After six months of sturm and drang she had to let him go. "I hated to do it," she said, "but I simply could not break him of the habit of rushing up to me in front of important visitors and calling me 'Mother Shapiro.' "

»»*««

WALTER WINCHELL attended a dinner party for which Beatrice Lillie (Lady Peel in private life) had trotted out the family pearls. A malicious rival murmured "I can't believe those pearls are genuine, my dear. They say you can always tell by biting them. Would you let me try?" "Certainly," said Miss Lillie promptly. "But remember, my sweet, that you can't tell real pearls with false teeth."

»»*««

A BEAUTIFUL young lady lay on a hospital bed, draped only in a bed-sheet. Two efficient-looking young men, dressed in white, approached, pulled back the sheet, and examined her with minute care. "Will you have to operate?" said the girl apprehensively. "You'll have to wait for the doctor to decide that," said one of the men. "We're only the house painters."

In Bob Hope's picture, "The Princess and the Pirate," the biggest laugh came when the pursuing galleon unfurled the skull and crossbones. "You know what that means?" said the Princess. "Sure," said Hope. "Iodine."

»» * ««

The first year that a group of Bahamian sportsmen introduced racing in Nassau, the spirit was willing but the horses were weak. The biggest horse on the entire island was about the size of a Shetland pony.

A racing card was scheduled for every Wednesday during the season. For the second meet, two gentlemen hired a rig to drive to the track. The driver let his horse amble along to suit itself. "We'd like to get to that track today, Driver," said one of the men. "Get a move on that nag." "No suh," said the driver firmly. "Dis hea horse am entered in the third race."

»» * ««

On Finnegan's first day as a regular on the police force, the Lieutenant told him, "Finnegan, I'm giving you an easy beat to start with—just from the station house to that red light and back." Finnegan disappeared for two days. "Where the devil were you?" roared the Lieutenant. "Didn't I tell you your beat was just from here to that red light?" "You did," agreed Finnegan, "but that red light was on the back of a truck."

»» * ««

Jack Benny says that he knows the only yes-man who ever dared to say "no" to a film magnate. The magnate asked him "Do you think there ever will be another producer with my genius?" The yes-man came through.

EARL WILSON was sent by his paper some years ago to cover an important story in Chicago. For four days his editor burned, because Wilson didn't file a single word. At last a wire from him arrived. The editor tore it open with trembling fingers. "Wire me two hundred dollars and my middle initial," it read. "I'm joining the Elks."

»»*««

THERE IS a famous broker in Wall Street whose name dare not be mentioned in this account. Sufficient it to say that on the day the market crashed in 1929, he was discovered astride his best customer after the close, prying the gold out of his teeth. One time he was captured in darkest Africa by twelve ferocious Zulus. He came back with eleven new margin accounts, and an order for Government bonds from the twelfth —the cautious witch doctor. He may have been slightly antique, but he was always in there pinching.

When a company was formed to finance a production of "The Miracle," this broker finally was caught off-base. He invested fifty thousand dollars in the venture. Norman Bel Geddes, a genius both at staging spectacles and spending money, transformed the entire Manhattan Opera House for this production. Rows of seats were ripped out, new lights and backdrops were installed, costs kept mounting. One night when the broker was attending rehearsal, Geddes suddenly decided the stage wasn't deep enough. A drill was installed, which promptly burst the water main on Thirty-Fourth Street. A stream of water shot twenty feet into the air. The broker let out a yell of jubilation. "Our fortunes are made," he cried. "Geddes has struck oil!"

THE LAST TIME Walter Clark, who wrote "The Ox-Bow Incident," visited my house, I told him the story of how Quentin Reynolds once won the intercollegiate plunging championship. Quent never had plunged in his life, but on the day of the meet, Brown's star plunger took sick and, in desperation, the Brown coach said, "Get me the biggest guy on the campus in his place." Quent was it. They filled him with Scotch, and when the gun barked, pushed him into the pool. By the time they hauled him out, slightly green around the edges, he had hit the opposite end of the tank and broken the distance record.

Clark was unimpressed. "We've got a fellow up in Cazenovia, New York," he said, "who is a *real* distance plunger. One day in Bar Harbor, Maine, he bet a fellow he could plunge all the way to Key West, Florida." "Did he win his bet?" I gasped. "Not only that," averred Clark, "but I guess he must have taken too deep a breath. He came up in the harbor of Rio de Janeiro."

»»∗««

"THAT CAZENOVIA lad had quite a way with the ladies, too," continued Clark. "He finally got killed in a hunting accident, and the story around our parts is that St. Peter turned a little pale when our friend presented himself at the Pearly Gates. 'Just a minute, my boy,' said St. Peter, and disappeared for some time. 'What's the idea?' said our boy when St. Peter came back. 'Don't I rate this place?' 'It wasn't that,' St. Peter assured him. 'I was just locking up all the women before I let you in.'"

"Walter," I said firmly, "I don't want to hear another word about that fellow from Cazenovia."

AN INTREPID big-game hunter was on his way back to camp with a record day's bag when a huge lion suddenly stalked out of the jungle not thirty paces away. The hunter had only one bullet left in his gun. He waited until the lion was ready to spring, took careful aim—and missed. The jig was up, he figured—but then a miracle occurred. The lion sprang too far, and landed in a heap fifteen feet beyond the hunter, who made the stockade in safety.

The next afternoon the hunter went into his back yard to practice a little shooting at close range. He heard a strange noise outside the fence, and peered over it to see what was afoot.

It was the lion—practicing short leaps!

»»*««

THE PRESENCE of that doughty martinet, Gen. Reginald Hotchkiss (retired) and his wife as guests of honor of the Hillsdale Country Club February 22 dinner dance was a source of deep pride to the socially ambitious president of that organization. Choking with self-importance and nervousness, he rose to introduce the General.

"Ladies n' genmen," he began, clearing his throat. "Our famous guest tonight bears a name familiar to you all. Its last syllable is what I hear he has given his wife every night for forty years. Here he is—that battle-scared—I mean bottle-scarred—I mean intrepid warrior, General Hotchkick. Er—pardon me, General—General Hotchkiss, of course. He will give us our Birthington's Washday—I mean Washington's Birthday address."

The General's own remarks were something of an anti-climax.

A HOLLYWOOD PRODUCER famous for unique use of the English language (this is one joke book that positively *will not* mention his name) recently startled an associate by the pronouncement, "It's no use trying to bury your head in an ostrich." The same gentleman's newest picture was produced in Pomona. The morning after, he met a competitor on Wilshire Boulevard and said "My picture last night was the most sensational success in the history of the industry. They wept like babies. They fell off their seats with laughter. I never saw anything like it." "Listen," said the competitor. "I happened to be at that prevue myself." "Oh," said the producer, his face falling. "But believe me, David, it's much better now."

»»*««

NOBODY COULD understand how a robust, hearty female like the Widow Cassidy could choose for her second husband a skinny little shrimp like Finnegan. Nor were they surprised when, after two years of henpecked existence, he quietly folded up and died. The night before the funeral, his wife, not too downcast, asked his friend Clancy to sit up with the body. "And mind ye don't go to slape in there," she warned. "The cat's dragged him out into the parlor twice already!"

»»*««

ED WYNN RECALLS that one of his first professional appearances was made as monologist in a gas-lit, outdoor amusement park. The applause, he says, wasn't terrific, but it was very steady; in fact, he began to hear scattered hand-claps almost as soon as he began his act. After his fifth bow, the stage manager hauled him off by the scuff of the neck. "They're not applauding you, you fool," he grumbled. "They're slapping mosquitoes!"

(224)

A MAN in the direct mail business, with an office on the fifty-third floor of the Chrysler Building, had an appointment with a Swedish farmer who wrote asking about agency rights in his remote corner of Minnesota. He was hours late, and arrived, dishevelled and out of breath, just as the direct-mail man was about to give him up as lost. "It bane one hell of a job to climb those stairs," he gasped. "Climb the stairs!" echoed the other. "Why on earth didn't you take the elevator?"

"I wanted to," said the Swede. "I ran for it, but I bane missed the damn thing!"

»»*««

AMERICAN AIRLINES reports that a lady taking her first plane ride was offered a stick of gum by the hostess. "It's for your ears," volunteered the latter. The passenger stopped her on her way through the cabin some minutes later. "It seems to be O.K." she reported, "but couldn't they find something a little less sticky?"

»»*««

OTTO KAHN, the late financier, once entertained a distinguished, and varied group of sophisticates aboard his yacht. After dinner, a discussion of the relative merits of different religious beliefs developed from a chance remark, and everybody got so excited and angry that they were astounded when one man happened to look at his watch and discovered it was 3 A.M. "Gentlemen," he said, "this is rather futile, I think. Let's get some sleep, and maybe we can resume this provocative discussing in the morning." Mr. Kahn banged his fist on the table. "No," he cried. "I propose that we stay up all night if necessary and settle this thing once and for all!"

(225)

"IN HOT SPRINGS, Arkansas," writes Amy Vanderbilt, "I saw some G.I.s goading the town's pet Indian—a venerable gent with two pigtails and a gold-toothed smile. "How do you like Hot Springs?" one of the G.I.s asked. "Well," replied the Indian, "We got rid of it, didn't we?"

»»*««

A FARM LAD was drafted. Home on his first furlough, he was asked what he thought of army life. "It's fine," he declared enthusiastically. "The food's good, the work's easy, and best of all, they let you sleep real late in the mornings."

»»*««

THE LATE King Edward VII, attending a royal conclave in Denmark, slipped off for a walk by himself one afternoon. He wandered further than he had intended, and was very happy to thumb a ride back in a farmer's hay wagon. "Drop me at the King's gatehouse," he told the farmer, who started with surprise, and asked "Who are you?" "I'm Edward VII of England," said the King simply. "Of course you are," roared the farmer, "and I'm the Pope."

After he had dropped his guest as requested, the farmer asked a servant, "Say, who is that man, anyhow?" "That's Edward VII," said the servant. The flabbergasted farmer scratched his head, and then told the servant, "You had better tell His Majesty that I, at least, was only fooling. I'm not the Pope at all!"

»»*««

"OUCH," cried Edgar Bergen. "I've got a splinter in my finger." "Oh, oh," commented Charlie McCarthy. "Anyone I know?"

(226)

WHEN JIMMY DURANTE came home from Alaska, he told of a sign he had seen outside an igloo which read, "Eskimo Spitz Dogs—Five Bucks A-piece." "What's so unusual about that?" somebody asked. "Unusual," exploded Jimmy. "I got fifty dollars that says the Eskimo can't do it!"

MRS. WILLIAMS was jubilant. "I've finally cured my husband of biting his nails," she declared. "Land sakes," said her neighbor. "How?" "I hide his teeth."

"I WONDER if you can locate my husband for me," a lady, just arrived in Heaven, asked wistfully of Saint Peter. "What's his name?" said St. Peter. "Bill Smith," said the lady. "My goodness, madam," Saint Peter declared patiently. "We have about four million Bill Smiths up here. Can't you think of some distinguishing characteristic?" "Well," mused the lady. "I do remember that just before he died, my Bill told me that if I ever was unfaithful to him, he'd turn in his grave." "That makes it simple," laughed Saint Peter. "Boy, go out and page Whirling Willie."

»»*««

A PATIENT LABORED industriously to convince his oculist that he saw things double. "There is no such malady," said the oculist firmly. "You've been drinking. When you sober up, everything will be O. K." "I was never more sober in my life," said the patient. "On the bus coming here, the girl sitting opposite me seemed like two girls. It's because I was seeing double." "Twins, no doubt," said the oculist. "I always eat one egg for breakfast," persisted the patient. "This morning I could have sworn there were two on the plate." "The waitress probably took pity on you," said the oculist. "And now I'll have to ask you to move on. I'm a busy man. The fee is ten dollars."

The patient threw a five-spot on the desk and said, "All right, smarty pants, have it your way."

»»*««

A BEAUTIFUL CLERK in a Hollywood bookstore told the boss, "I need a holiday. I look terrible." "Nonsense," laughed the boss. "It's not nonsense," insisted the clerk. "The male customers are beginning to count their change."

(228)

George Jessel says that when *he* first broke in his act, he had the misfortune to follow one of the biggest flops in the history of Loew's 116th Street Theatre. "They were still hissing when I walked onto the stage," Jessel declares. "I was so good that for a couple of minutes I held them enthralled, but about half way through my second song they remembered how mad they had been and started hissing that last act all over again!"

»»*««

That story reminds me of my favorite Al Smith anecdote.

The Governor was one of a party of twenty convivials at a mid-winter weekend at Walter Jacobs' beautiful Lake Tarleton Club in New Hampshire. This is a tremendously popular summer resort, but in winter it is a pretty lonely spot. Jacobs opened it specially for this occasion. On Sunday, Al Smith and the two other Catholics in the party got up at four-thirty to drive a full twenty miles to six o'clock mass. It was pitch black and about thirty degrees below zero. The Governor bundled himself into about four sweaters and a fur-lined coat, took a last wistful look at his non-Catholic friends sleeping peacefully, and murmured as he stepped out into the snow, "Wouldn't it be awful if it turned out that they were right and we were wrong!"

»»*««

A persistent salesman was ushered into a powerful tycoon's private sanctum at the tag end of a hectic day. "It speaks well for your power of persuasion that you wangled your way in here," said the tycoon. "I've refused to see fourteen other important agents today." "I know," said the salesman. "I'm all of them."

THE F.B.I. wanted a fugitive very badly on charges of murder, rape, arson, and a few other minor technicalities. They collected six old pictures of him, and rushed them to police all over the country. Shortly thereafter, a small-town constable wired "Hereby acknowledge receipt of pictures of the six birds you're looking for. Happy to say we've got five of them already rounded up and are hot on the trail of the sixth."

»»*««

NORMAN COUSINS, editor of the Saturday Review of Literature, came home from Washington with the story of a golf match between Supreme Court Justice Stone and a distinguished Virginia bishop. The bishop missed four straight shots in a bunker without saying a single word. Justice Stone watched him with some amusement and remarked, "Bishop, that is the most profane silence I ever heard."

»»*««

THE BOSTON TRANSCRIPT, forced to suspend publication some years ago, because of public indifference, once stood high in the ranks of the country's newspapers. Among Boston's own Brahmins and blue-bloods it was in a class by itself. A Beacon Hill butler is reported once to have come to his employer and announced, "Sir, two reporters and a gentleman from the Transcript are outside to see you." The paper died because the younger generation would have none of it. Kenneth Stewart writes that in its last days it received a letter which read, "Please cancel our subscription. Grandma just died."

(230)

WHEN MOSS HART signed up to tour the Far East in his own "The Man Who Came to Dinner," he grew a beard for the purpose. His brother Bernie, encountering him unexpectedly when the whiskers were a mere four-inch bristle, recoiled in horror and exclaimed, "You couldn't have been born! You were trapped!"

»»*««

PAUL ROBESON's triumphal portrayal of "Othello" stirred an old ham in the audience to a bit of reminiscing during the second intermission. "I shall never forget the day," he announced in a whisper that could be heard within a radius of two square blocks, "the time Boothe played Hamlet to my grave-digger. Ah, gentleman, what a cast that was!"

»»*««

THE LATE Aimee Semple McPherson really slipped into high gear when the plate was being passed around. "Contribute to the cause," she would chant. "Make your donation to the good fight lest you spend eternity roasting in hell, a-wailing, and a-suffering, and a-gnashing of your teeth." "Sister," protested one not-entirely converted soul, "I can't never be a-gnashin' of my teeth because I plumb ain't got any." "Teeth," said Aimee sharply, "will be provided."

»»*««

A RURAL NEWSPAPER in Alabama reports the story of an old Negro who was out fishing when a huge tarpon caught his hook and yanked him overboard. The startled fisherman came to the surface and spluttered, "What I cain't figger out, is dis nigger a-fishin' or is dis fish a-niggerin'?"

(231)

BETTY SMITH, who wrote the book about that tree in Brooklyn, says that when an optimist declares "This is the best of all possible worlds," it's the dyed-in-the-wool pessimist who always answers "You're probably right."

»»*««

A CAPTAIN in an infantry unit made up for the most part of draftees from the Cicero district of Chicago summoned one of his lieutenants. "Better look up the pre-induction record of Private Spotts," he said. "I've noticed that every time he fires his pistol on the range he wipes off the finger-marks!"

»»*««

A HOT DISPUTE between three tough young marines—two from Brooklyn, the other from a farm in Tennessee—is reported by Emory Ferree, a Field Director of the American Red Cross. The Brooklyn boys were brazenly essaying to tell the one from Tennessee how a farm really should be run. It was their interesting contention that the only reason a farmer had a hard life was because of his stubborn insistence about keeping cows. "Ya gotta milk 'em before daylight in the morning and after dark at night. If it wasn't for that ya could live like a reg'lar human bein'," declared one. The farm boy waved his head in negation and tried to explain, but with his Southern drawl he wasn't able to get two words out before the other Brooklyn expert had the floor. "Why in hell can't some smart feller make them cows give milk in daylight?" he demanded. His buddy promptly answered, "Not a chance. They're too damn modest." Ferree says that at this point the Tennessean swallowed his chew and clutched feebly for the rail of the ship.

(232)

A SMALL-TOWN editor once made the mistake of feuding with the great American humorist, George Ade, and threatened, "I'm going to expose you in my next week's issue." "Go as far as you like," said Ade genially. "I can walk clear outside of your circulation in four minutes flat."

Ade's most successful play was "The College Widow." His mother came to see it one night and said, "George, do you really get more than $500 a week for doing that?" "Yes, mother," answered Ade. "George," she said earnestly, "you keep right on fooling them."

»»*««

SID SKOLSKY, peer of Hollywood correspondents, tells the story of Errol Flynn's first meeting with Lily Damita. It was a chilly afternoon at the Hearst ranch. Flynn was seated in the library. Miss Damita brushed by him without so much as a smile and tried to warm herself in front of the open fire. Flynn watched her rocking back and forth in silence for a few minutes and then said, "Pardon, lady, but if that's for me, not too-well-done, please."

»»*««

JACK DOUGLAS, Hollywood scripter, declares that between halves of the last Rose Bowl game, his uncle walked to the middle of the field, looked over the 90,000 fans, pulled out a gun and snapped, "Don't anybody move—this is a stick-up."

»»*««

AN OFFICIAL in a big Hollywood studio, checking office life insurance applications, came across one in which an employee named his girl friend beneficiary, and then filled out the space headed "relationship to you" with the word "nice."

(233)

PHIL BAKER claims that he knows a little blonde who answers to the name of Sugar-plum Jefferson. She can swing a "yo-all" and a "honey chile" with the best of them, although she was born in Canarsie. It seems she acquired her Southern accent by drinking out of a Dixie Cup.

Sugar-plum gave up eating grapefruit when they started putting cherries on the top. "Ah never paid no mind when the grapefruit squirted in mah lil old eye," she explained, "but when it started shootin' cannon balls, that was too much."

»»✳««

AN ALMOST unbelievable story of Portuguese muddling in the days before a strong dictatorship was clamped upon the country concerns a sudden decision to build a miniature "Maginot Line" along the Spanish border. A special tax was levied on the entire nation to pay for this wall and all the country's best engineers combined forces to make it "impregnable." The work went forward and all Portugal puffed with satisfaction as the huge guns were wheeled into place and pill-box after pill-box was erected, bristling with defensive apparatus of every sort. The day for the dedication of the line came amid universal rejoicing, but suddenly somebody made a horrible discovery. Every gun and every defense mechanism had been built facing Portugal instead of Spain. There was a series of explosive consultations in which many picturesque Portuguese epithets filled the air, but something was saved out of the wreckage after all. A slick Portuguese businessman sold the whole defense line to Spain—at 30¢ on the dollar.

THE CONCORD BOOKSHOP staff is still puzzling over an episode that occurred during last year's Christmas rush. A lady and her daughter asked for a book on boat building. The clerk showed them Chapelle's standard volume, but the $5.00 price tag bothered them "Phone papa," said the lady, "and see if he is willing to spend that much." The daughter reported in due course, "Papa says the hell with it. You should buy a Hershey bar instead."

»»*««

"I THINK I can explain why my husband feels down in the mouth," said a housewife thoughtfully. "I forgot to take the feathers off the duck we had for dinner."

»»*««

GERTRUDE STEIN's publisher once sent her a royalty check for "two thousand thousand dollars dollars" and signed it "Random is a Random is a House." Miss Stein returned the check with the angry command, "Cut this nonsense and make my check out properly."

»»*««

BRANCH CABELL points out that old General Nathan Forrest knew how to cut straight through Army red tape. The Richmond Museum treasures a document in which an Army captain made a formal request for leave. On the back of it, the forthright General scrawled his reply: "I tol you twict, Consarn it, No!"

»»*««

JONATHAN WHITE, single, well-to-do, and thirty-five, lived peacefully at the Methodist Sisters' Boarding House until the night the alert lady in charge heard him drop his shoes on the floor twice.

(235)

WHEN THE YANKS captured Bonn, hundreds of them dropped in to rubber at the home of Beethoven, long a museum, and miraculously undamaged by bombardment. A cocky sergeant, who had been a member of a jazz band before the war, caught sight of the piano at which Beethoven composed his Fifth Symphony, jumped over the red ribbon that guarded it, and played "Rum and Coca-Cola" with one finger. "I guess every pianist who comes into this joint plays something on that pianner," he said to the old guide. "Not quite," said the guide. "When Paderewski was here, he said it would be sacrilege if he touched it!"

»»＊««

A WEALTHY but unprincipled playwright declared himself in on a regular Monday night poker session which some of the town's leading authors, producers, and actors have conducted for years. The playwright lost several hundred dollars, and then welched on the debt.

Recently a new play he had written opened on Broadway, and laid a magnificent egg. Just before the final curtain, a rat scampered across the stage. Two members of the poker club jumped up and yelled "author! author!"

»»＊««

A MAN fell overboard from a Caribbean liner and screamed for help when he saw a school of man-eating sharks heading in his direction. A famous criminal lawyer called "I'll help you." He dove into the ocean. The sharks immediately formed a two-lane escort and convoyed the two men back to the boat. "It's a miracle," cried the rescued man. "Not at all," said the lawyer. "Mere professional courtesy, that's all."

(236)

JOHN STEINBECK tells a story about an old, retired sea-dog with a peg leg, who made his headquarters on a wharf at Monterey and was regarded as one of the chief points of interest of the town by visitors. The latter learned very quickly to observe the tradition of holding up before the old salt a $5.00 bill in one hand and a quarter in the other and offering him his choice. Invariably, the simple old fellow's face lit up with joy and, without hesitation, he chose the quarter. The tourists all went away vastly gratified.

One blustery day, when there was nobody else in sight, Steinbeck engaged the old salt in conversation. "Gimpy," he said, "I am really surprised at you. Don't you know by this time that a $5.00 bill is worth exactly twenty times as much as a quarter, no matter how shiny and silvery the latter may be?"

Gimpy gave him an elaborate wink and cackled, "Of course I do, Skipper. But if I ever once chose a $5.00 bill, the jig would be up forever."

»»✳«««

THE DONNEGAN BROTHERS were dining in a strange roof-garden. Tim went to wash up, and was directed to a door to the left of the elevator. "Go down two steps and there you are," said the head-waiter. Tim unfortunately forgot to turn to the left. He opened the elevator door, took one step down, and promptly fell down the shaft.

The Donnegans came from hardy stock, and Tim was merely stunned. When his brother Mike rose to wash up, however, Tim cautioned him, "Look out for that second step, Mike—it's a son-of-a-gun!"

(237)

FRED ALLEN and his wife Portland were strolling down Eighth Avenue when Fred spotted a sign that read "Barnum and Bailey." "I'll have to go there," announced Fred. "When those two fellows get together, it's a circus." "Better take these cheese sandwiches with you," suggested Portland. "What's the idea?" quoth Fred. "Mementoes to take to the circus?" "Two of them are mementoes," said Portland. "The rest are camembert."

»»*««

"WHY DOES a chicken cross the road?"

"That wasn't no chicken—that was my wife."

Index

Geese (and Ganders), 126, 142
Genealogist (definition), 185
Generosity, 160
Gentlemen only, 60, 185
Genuine article, 53
Getting up at Night, 82
Gibbs, Wolcott, 208
G. I. Humor, 131, 226, 236
Girls, Big and Little, 26, 41, 98, 100, 106,
   115, 122, 178
Godowski, Leopold, 132
Golf, 5, 16, 24, 52, 80, 150, 152, 161, 165,
   177, 205, 230
Good Manners (definition), 185
Gossamer (definition), 185
Grable, Betty, 2
Grammar, 146
Grand Central Station, 158
Grandfather, 149
Grandmother, 57, 90, 146
Greek, 210
Grocery Stores, 62, 142
Guinea Pigs, 127

Ham, 73, 150
Hard of hearing, 214
Harem, 73
Hart, Moss, 231
Harvard, 172
Hay, Jan, 186
Health, 51, 103, 109
Held, Anna, 201
Hell, 152, 231
Hemingway, Ernest, 61
Henpecked, 118, 132
Herford, Oliver, 186
Hershfield, Harry, 118
Hillbilly Humor, 92, 114, 118, 133, 142,
   165, 178
History (definition), 186
Hoboes, 27, 131
Hollywood, 2, 6, 21, 91, 102, 153, 162, 164,
   201, 202, 205, 220, 224, 228, 233
Holtz, Lou, 32, 219
Holy Water, 108
Honeymoons, 1, 68, 106, 135
Hope, Bob, 205 220
Horse and Buggy, 65, 171
Horse meat, 79
Horseradish, 149
Horses, 2, 4, 11, 28, 55, 68, 95, 124, 125,
   137, 171, 220
Hospital humor, 81, 219
Hospitality, 5, 15, 158
Hotel humor, 7, 22, 51, 54, 64, 66, 68, 83,
   90, 93, 175
Housepainter, 50, 130, 219
Huebsch, Ben, 158
Hunting, 99, 127, 223
Hurley, Pat, 118
Hurricane, 177
Hysterics, 141

Iceman, 4, 85, 146
Ignorance, 178
Impertinence, 158
Income Tax, 54, 67
Incongruous (definition), 186
Incriminating Evidence, 116
Indian, 145, 226
Insomnia, 132
Installments, 90
Insurance, 107, 112, 233
Intentions, 165
Interest, 94
Interruptions, 86
Interview, 125
Invention, 170
Iodine, 220
Irish humor, 18, 23, 53, 58, 68, 82, 97, 99,
   107, 108, 112, 129, 140, 149, 159, 167, 214,
   220, 224, 237
Italian humor, 3, 4

Janitor, 53
Jeep, 80
Jerk, 202
Jersey mosquitoes, 66
Jessel, George, 28, 108, 110, 122, 229
Jewels, 65, 135, 175, 185, 219
Jewish Humor, 5, 12, 22, 46, 53, 71, 76, 82,
   89, 94, 96, 103, 118, 124, 130, 141, 150,
   152, 154, 158, 171, 218
Job, 145
Johnson, Nunnally, 42
Jolson, Al, 108
Journalism, 156
Judge, 79, 81, 106, 111, 150, 160
Juries, 40
Juveniles, 2, 44, 46, 50, 56, 58, 69, 76, 96,
   98, 121, 145, 146, 152, 161, 169, 170, 174,
   175, 179, 205, 208

Kahn, Otto M., 225
Kangaroo, 219
Keyhole, 57, 201
Kids, 31, 34, 41, 50, 76, 172
Kings, 128, 226
Kisses, 10, 69, 80, 126, 186, 203
Knot holes, 178
Kober, Arthur, 103

Ladder, 50, 58, 79, 129
La Guardia, Mayor, 55
Lamarr, Hedy, 201
Lamas, 155
L'amour, 64
Lap, 212
Lardner, Ring, 178
Lauder, Harry, 8
Laundry, 143
Lawyers, 26, 40, 50, 79, 117, 129, 149, 174,
   203, 208, 218, 236
Leacock, Stephen, 151
Lear, Edward, 191

(241)